D0483916

Travels with

HENRY JAMES

HENRY JAMES

Foreword by
HENDRIK HERTZBERG

Introduction by
MICHAEL ANESKO

NATION
BOOKS
New York

Published by Nation Books, an imprint of Perseus Books, LLC,
a subsidiary of Hachette Book Group, Inc. 116 East 16th Street, 8th Floor,
New York, NY 10003

Nation Books is a co-publishing venture of the
Nation Institute and Perseus Books

Books published by Nation Books are available at special discounts for bulk
purchases in the United States by corporations, institutions, and other
organizations. For more information, please contact the Special Markets
Department at the Perseus Books Group, 2300 Chestnut Street, Suite 200,
Philadelphia, PA 19103, or call (800) 810-4145, ext. 5000, or e-mail special.
markets@perseusbooks.com.

Designed by Trish Wilkinson

The photograph of Henry James on the jacket was taken from the frontispiece
of *Short Story Classics (American)*, Volume Three, ed. William Patten, copyright
© 1905, printed by P.F. Collier & Son. Photographer unknown. *Wikimedia*.

A CIP catalog record for this book is available from the Library of Congress.
ISBN: 978-1-56858-577-2 (hardcover)
ISBN: 978-1-56858-578-9 (e-book)

10 9 8 7 6 5 4 3 2 1

CONTENTS

Contents

FOREWORD

Hendrik Hertzberg

H ENRY JAMES WAS A COCKSURE FREELANCER OF TWENTY-two
when he published, in the November 16, 1865, issue of a
four-month-old weekly called *The Nation*, one of American literature's most notorious pans.[*] He judged a book he anony-
mously reviewed—*Drum-Taps*, a collection of what he dismissed
as "spurious poetry"—"an offense against art," "clumsy," "monstrous," devoid of "common sense," and "aggressively careless,
inelegant, and ignorant." Having laid the groundwork, the future author of *The Portrait of a Lady*, *Daisy Miller*, *The Ambassadors*, *The Golden Bowl*, *The Turn of the Screw*, and much, much
more, proceeded to address himself directly to the offending
versifier, scolding him as follows: "To become adopted as a

---

[*] Henry James, "Mr. Walt Whitman," *Nation* 1 (November 16, 1865):
1:625–626.

national poet, it is not enough to discard everything in particular and to accept everything in general, to amass crudity upon crudity, to discharge the undigested contents of your blotting-book into the lap of the public. You must respect the public you address; for it has taste, if you have not. . . . It is not enough to be rude, lugubrious, and grim. You must also be serious."

Forgive him. He was young and full of beans. In time, of course, Henry James would change his mind about Walt Whitman—so much so that by 1904, he and Edith Wharton were spending long evenings joyously reading to each other from *Leaves of Grass*. (As James read, Wharton would recall, "his voice filled the hushed room like an organ adagio," and he exclaimed, "Oh, yes, a great genius, undoubtedly a very great genius!"*) At about the same time, in a letter to a friend who had teased him about that long-ago review, he was theatrically contrite. It was a "disgrace," he lamented, a "little atrocity" that he had "perpetrated [on Whitman] in the gross impudence of youth." He added, "I only know that I haven't seen the accursed thing for more than thirty years, and that if it were to cross my path nothing would induce me to look at it. I am so far from 'keeping' the abominations of my early innocence that I destroy

---

*Leon Edel, *Henry James: A Life* (New York: Harper & Row, 1985), 599.

them whenever I spy them—which, thank goodness, occurs rarely."*

Thank goodness the mature James was in no position to destroy his youthful abominations, none of which, by the way, were abominable. (Even his rash demolition of Whitman crackles with thrilling exuberance.) The travel pieces collected here make the case. Besides being delightful in their own right, these youthful nonabominations are important for what they presage. They are among the first stirrings of a great career with few parallels among American and British writers—or among writers of any nationality, for that matter—of the period between the American Civil War and World War I. (For literature, the Gilded Age was twenty-four-carat gold.)

Samuel Johnson's immortal wisecrack—"No man but a blockhead ever wrote, except for money"—didn't apply to Henry James. Not quite, anyway. Strictly speaking, James didn't "need" money. His father, Henry James Sr., had inherited the equivalent today of some $8 million and was generally willing to supply a letter of credit whenever one of his children was short of ready cash. Henry Jr. loved his father and mother and his brothers and sister, but he also loved independence. He wanted

---

*Henry James to Manton Marble, October 10, 1903, in *Henry James: Selected Letters*, ed. Leon Edel (Cambridge, MA: Harvard University Press, 1987), 348.

only to write, and he wanted to write what he wanted to write, and he wanted to go where he wanted to go, and he wanted to answer to no one but himself. Ultimately, he wrote to make art. But he also wrote to unencumber himself, to free himself to make art. He wrote to write. For him, writing was its own purpose—but not its only purpose, not every time he sat down at his writing table.

In an era when relatively few members of the literate middle- and upper-middle classes could afford to travel for pleasure, touring by surrogate was the next best thing. There was a healthy market for travel writing. It was a circulation builder, and the magazines were eager to cash in. Even a small, intellectually elite journal like *The Nation*—which, then as now, lived for politics, with a sideline in cultural criticism—wanted in on the action.

In a modest way, so did James. Money seldom motivates writers at today's *Nation*, but for James at yesterday's, it was high on the list. The fees he earned for these pieces—$50 each—may not sound like much, but they were enough to take him much of the way toward self-sufficiency as he meandered through the northeastern United States, Britain, and Western Europe during the 1870s, piling up impressions that, sooner or later, would turn up in his novels and stories.

Henry James was, almost literally, a born traveler. He was barely six months old in October 1843, when, with his family, he crossed the Atlantic for the first time. (The Jameses went in style, aboard the *Great Western*, a paddle-wheel, wooden-hulled steamship of unprecedented size and luxury.) He made four more crossings in his teens, attending a bewildering variety of schools, studying with a succession of private tutors, and making of himself a bilingual habitué of London, Paris, and Geneva. In the 1860s he was back in the United States, mostly in Boston and Cambridge. He didn't return to Europe until 1869, this time as a full-grown man and emphatically on his own, for fifteen months of intensive travel—London again, Paris again, Geneva again, and then, in a state of something like ecstasy, Italy: Milan, Verona, Padua, Venice, Pisa, Naples, Genoa, Florence, and Rome.

When he came home again to Cambridge, he was twenty-seven. He had not yet written a book and was not yet famous, but his reviews and stories had made him a favorite of the editors of the better magazines. Leon Edel, the definitive James biographer, summarizes his subject's next move—and the motives behind it:

> He was barely resettled in Quincy Street in the early summer of 1870 when he persuaded *The Nation* to accept a series of travel articles from his pen—pictures of Rhode Island, Vermont, New York. It was an opportunity to earn some ready money; it was also a way of convincing *The Nation* how lively a travel writer he could be—especially if he were in Europe.

There was, however, a deeper prompting. He would be "haunted and wracked," he told [his dear friend] Grace Norton, if he returned to Europe with a "thankless ignorance and neglect" of his homeland. He would therefore "see all I can of America and *rub it in* with unfaltering zeal." His tour consisted of a month in Saratoga, where he drank the waters and "cunningly noted many of the idiosyncrasies of American civilization"; a week at Lake George; a fortnight at Pomfret, where his parents were on holiday; and a fortnight at Newport."*

At least three things are especially striking about this: First, young James considers himself enough of a stranger in the land of his birth that he feels obliged to undertake a field trip, a systematic program of self-education aimed at familiarizing himself with its physical and social features. Second, he proposes to tour an extraordinarily narrow slice of his country. In order to "see all I can of America," he draws up an itinerary consisting entirely of prosperous resort communities in the Northeast. Third, in addition to boning up on "America" and earning a bit of money, he aims to induce *The Nation* to subsidize his travel in Europe, the place for which his zeal was truly unfaltering. His six *Nation*

---

* Edel, *Henry James*, 119–120.

essays on American places leverage seventeen more from England, Scotland, France, Germany, and, most lovingly, Italy.

Edel's snapshot provides a glimpse of the strategic genius of James's generalship of his career. From the beginning, he marched toward greatness in stately fashion, according to an inner schedule. His ambition was vast, his confidence in his art and ability unfathomable. He was his own teacher, his own mentor, his own critic, his own taskmaster. The ultimate result, over time, was a body of work unmatched for filigreed quality as well as sheer quantity. (In the stacks of the Dartmouth College library, I found twenty-five feet of shelf space devoted to the writings of Henry James, with another twenty feet holding books about him.) By the end of the decade during which these essays were written, James would emerge, at thirty-seven, as the mature literary master he would remain for the second half of his life.

For readers of these Jamesian postcards, then and now, there is welcome relief from the news of the day. The tribulations of war and politics and revolution almost never intrude, and when they do, it is only in a passing reference or offhand phrase. At his Lake George hotel in 1870, relaxing with the New York papers, he is "reading of the great deeds of Prussia and the confusion of France" while listening to a German American marching band. "What an omen for the Prussian future!" he marvels. "Their simple Teutonic presence seemed a portent." (How much of a portent he could not know.) In Paris in 1872, "after a busy, dusty, weary day in the streets, staring at charred ruins and finding in all things a vague aftertaste of gunpowder," he attends a Molière comedy at the Théâtre Français. The magnificence of the performance prompts him to feel "a sort of languid ecstasy of contemplation and wonder—wonder that the tender flower of poetry and art should bloom again so bravely over blood-stained garments and fresh-made graves." (He is alluding to the brutal suppression of the Paris Commune the year before.) But we are not on an earnest fact-finding trip in these essays. We're not down and out in Paris and London. No, we are up and away in Saratoga and Venice (and Paris and London too). We are traveling for pleasure, and pleasure is what James gives us—pleasure in the places he takes us and, above all, the pleasure of his company.

To travel with James in these pages is to take an unhurried vacation with a thoroughly seasoned, supremely cultivated, acutely intelligent companion. Our guide is a curious, engaged observer not only of landscapes and streets and cathedrals but also of paintings and plays and the characteristics—national, social, and individual—of the people we encounter at his side. This is a book to read slowly, the better to absorb its sights and sounds, its insights and reflections—a book of walks, with now and then a ride in a horse-drawn carriage, hooves rattling on cobblestones. Word by word, phrase by phrase, James's long, purposefully meandering, beautifully detailed sentences will guide you around the curves of a country road, up the steps of a moldering castle, into the quiet of a rural inn or the bustle of a grand hotel. Take the advice of your traveling companion:

> To walk in quest of any object that one has more or less ten-derly dreamed of—to find your way—to steal upon it softly—to see at last, if it is church or castle, the tower-tops peeping above elms or beeches—to push forward with a rush, and emerge, and pause, and draw that first long breath which is the compromise between so many sensations—this is a pleasure left to the tourist even after the broad glare of photography has dissipated so many of the sweet mysteries of travel.

So pack your bags. Don't forget your pocket watch, your deerstalker hat or bonnet, and your steamship tickets. Here's your Baedeker. *Bon voyage!*

INTRODUCTION: A LITTLE TOUR WITH HENRY JAMES

Michael Anesko

MOST PEOPLE WHO KNOW SOMETHING OF HENRY JAMES might also know that, shortly before his death in 1916, he succumbed to a series of debilitating strokes. In their wake, for weeks he drifted in and out of consciousness, but often still capable of speech. While his faithful amanuensis, Theodora Bosanquet, remained with him, she dutifully recorded the words he spoke—as she had for years, seated at a Remington type-writer while he dictated the texts of his late fiction and much of his voluminous correspondence. In the latter of these frag-mentary transcripts from his subconscious, Henry James trans-ported himself back to France—even assuming the name of Napoléone—and declared his ambition to renovate certain apartments of the Louvre and the Tuileries, a grand project that would possess "a majesty unsurpassed by any work of the kind yet undertaken" in the First Empire.[*] In the strange meandering of his stricken brain, Henry James was completing a lifetime circuit of travel, for his very earliest memory[†] was of sitting in a carriage—at two years of age—waggling his small feet under a flowing robe and taking in "the admirable aspect of the Place and the Colonne Vendôme,"[‡] a monument erected in 1810 to commemorate Napoleon Bonaparte's crushing victories at Austerlitz and Jena. Paris, of course, would provide the setting for some of the Master's finest work—*The Ambassadors* (1903), perhaps most notably—but, almost from the beginning, his long shelf of stories and novels mapped out a crisscrossing itinerary of transatlantic scope, often in tandem with his own peripatetic adventures.

Not long after James's birth in a house off Washington Square in New York City, his restless father (and namesake) took the family abroad for two years, first to Paris and then to London. The Jameses then spent the next ten years back in the United States, sometimes in Albany—where the paternal

---

[*] Henry James, "The Deathbed Dictation," in *Henry James Letters*, ed. Leon Edel, 4 vols. (Cambridge, MA: Belknap Press of Harvard University Press, 1974–1984), 4:811.

[†] Disclosed in the first of his autobiographical volumes, Henry James, *A Small Boy and Others*, ed. Peter Collister (1913; rpt. Charlottesville: University of Virginia Press, 2011).

[‡] James, *A Small Boy and Others*, 46.

grandfather had made a vast fortune—but mostly on the island of Manhattan, whose bustling streets, theaters, and museums afforded the growing boy a prime urban spectacle. Ever wary of our native fixation on business and moneymaking, the elder Henry James still wanted to give his children (as he told Ralph Waldo Emerson) "a better sensuous education" than they were likely to receive in America,* and so he packed the family off again to Europe and distributed his brood, at various times, among schools in Geneva, London, Paris, Boulogne-sur-Mer, and Bonn or hired tutors to proctor them at home as they moved from place to place. Suckled thus in cosmopolitanism, young Henry James was never weaned.

At the age of twenty-six, Henry James Jr. (as he was then known) had already begun a literary career by writing short fiction and noticing current books for periodicals such as the *North American Review*, *The Atlantic*, and *The Nation*. At this point, he made his first solo trip abroad, deliberately choosing to follow an itinerary of his own making. His parents and older brother, William, had wanted him to absorb the rigors of German philosophy (and the tortuosities of the German language), but instead, after spending several months in England, France, and Switzerland,

---

*Henry James Sr. to Ralph Waldo Emerson, August 31, 1849, in Ralph Barton Perry, *The Thought and Character of William James*, 2 vols. (Boston: Little, Brown, 1935) 1:59.

young Henry James crossed the Alps on foot and descended into Italy—a country and a culture still foreign to him, as his parents had never ventured there on any of the family's previous European forays. Voluminous letters back to Cambridge chart the progress of his travels—as well as his burgeoning enthusiasm. Upon reaching the Eternal City, he gushed, "At last—for the first time—I live! It beats everything: it leaves the Rome of your fancy—your education—nowhere. It makes Venice—Florence—Oxford—London—seem like little cities of pasteboard. I went reeling and moaning thro' the streets, in a fever of enjoyment."* With time, those other places easily regained their luster in the young writer's estimation, and the consecrated experience of them reaffirmed what would become the touchstones of travel for James: close observation, judicious measure, and comparison.

In 1872, James again had occasion to travel abroad, this time as a male guide and chaperone for his younger sister Alice (1848–1892) and their maternal "Aunt Kate" (Catharine Walsh, 1812–1889). After accompanying the women that summer to what was by then an almost familiar series of destinations in England, France, Switzerland, and Italy, James followed them to Liverpool in October to get them aboard a steamer heading

---

*Henry James to William James, October 30, [1869], Edel, *Henry James Letters*, 1:160.

back to America. But now he was determined to stay on and prove to himself (and his overstretched parents!) that he could support himself by his pen and not rely on banker's drafts from Cambridge to pay for his sojourn. Most of the pieces reprinted in this volume provide fruitful testimony to that ambition as well as confirmation that he could. A quick census of his serial publications from 1872 through 1874 yields a fulsome tally: in those three years he published no fewer than eight short stories, seven notices of art installations or gallery exhibitions, twenty-eight book or theater reviews, and thirty travel sketches. Hardly an idle traveler, Henry James worked at his desk almost everywhere he went.

In many of these travel pieces we can catch humorous glimpses of details and elements that would find their way into James's later works of fiction. In Saratoga, for example, the writer is forever being reminded that the superlative seems to be the natural degree of American idiom. "The piazza of the Union Hotel, I have been repeatedly informed, is the largest 'in the world.'" His own broader experience obliges James to qualify such claims by gentle comparison: "There are a number of objects in Saratoga, by the way, which in their respective kinds are the finest in the world. One of these is Mr. John Morrissey's casino. I bowed my head submissively to this statement, but privately I thought of the blue Mediterranean, and the little white promontory of Monaco, and the silver-gray verdure of olives, and the view across the outer sea toward the bosky cliffs of Italy."

In *Daisy Miller* we hear such national braggadocio coming even from the mouths of babes: despite the loss of most of his baby teeth to dental caries, young Randolph Miller still insists that "American candy's the best candy," preferring it to lumps of sugar from the table d'hôte of the Trois Couronnes at Vevey.* In *The Portrait of a Lady*, the irrepressible New York journalist Henrietta Stackpole finds nothing in Europe that can stack up against American counterexamples: neither London nor Paris nor Rome can match "the luxury of our western cities," she proudly boasts; even the majestic dome of St. Peter's suffers "by comparison with that of the Capitol at Washington."† How could Michelangelo hold a candle to Thomas U. Walter?

Subscribers to the *Nation* also might have appreciated the author's subtle inside joking, when in 1870 he echoed a phrase first coined in the pages of the journal not long before. Strolling along the main avenue of Burlington, Vermont, James is favor-

---

*Henry James, "Daisy Miller: A Study," in *Complete Stories, 1874–1884* (New York: Library of America, 1999), 240.

†Henry James, *The Portrait of a Lady*, in *Novels, 1881–1886* (New York: Library of America, 1985), 413, 493.

ably impressed by "the pleasant, solid American homes, with their blooming breadth of garden, sacred with peace and summer and twilight." One of them in particular strikes his fancy, but he coyly defers ampler description of its domestic charm: "I reserve it for its proper immortality in the first chapter of the great American novel." We must credit another *Nation* writer, John W. De Forest, with that legendary formulation; his brief essay, "The Great American Novel," appeared in one of the earliest issues of 1868.*

But James redeemed this playful promise by using just such a setting in the first chapter of his (would-be) "great American novel," *Roderick Hudson* (1875), which opens with a modest widow "doing the honors of an odorous cottage on a midsummer evening," entertaining a visitor on "the rose-framed porch" of her comfortable home in Northampton, Massachusetts.† When, again in "Newport," James "can almost imagine . . . a transient observer of the Newport spectacle dreaming momentarily of a great American novel, in which the heroine shall be infinitely realistic, and yet neither a schoolmistress nor an outcast," he might even be anticipating the type of female

---

* John W. De Forest, "The Great American Novel," *Nation* 6 (January 9, 1868): 27–29.

† Henry James, *Roderick Hudson*, in *Novels, 1871–1880* (New York: Library of America, 1983), 168.

protagonist that would become the consistent hallmark of his most enduring early work: Daisy Miller, in that eponymous novella, Catherine Sloper of *Washington Square* (1880), and Isabel Archer of *The Portrait of a Lady* (1881).

To be sure, an intelligent appreciation of travel encouraged Henry James to put a high premium on the virtues of literary realism. It is worth mentioning that his other notable contemporaries, Mark Twain and William Dean Howells, also spent formative years in Europe at the earliest stages of their respective careers—an experience that keenly sharpened their awareness of distinctive cultural traits, manners, and habits of speech and helped them to dispel the kinds of romanticized impressions to which "innocents abroad" especially were prone.

Likewise wary of that tendency, James famously acknowledged (in an 1872 letter), "It's a complex fate, being an American, and one of the responsibilities it entails is fighting against a superstitious valuation of Europe."* The experience of travel was, perhaps, the best safeguard. As James concluded in "Homburg Reformed" (1873), "The observations of the 'cultivated American' bear chiefly, I think, upon the great topic of national idiosyncrasies. He is apt to have a keener sense of them than Europeans; it matters more to his imagination that his neighbor

---

*Henry James to Charles Eliot Norton, February 4, 1872, in Edel, *Henry James Letters*, 1:274.

is English, French, or German. He often seems to me to be a creature wandering aloof, but half naturalized himself. His neighbors are outlined, defined, imprisoned, if you will, by their respective national moulds, pleasing or otherwise; but his own type has not hardened yet into the Old-World bronze."

In his travel writing collected here, as elsewhere, the touchstone for Henry James is freedom.

SARATOGA

August 3, 1870

Map of Saratoga Springs, ca. 1888.

ONE HAS VAGUE IRRESPONSIBLE LOCAL PREVISIONS OF which it is generally hard to discern the origin. You find yourself thinking of an unknown, unseen place as thus rather than so. It assumes in your mind a certain shape, a certain color which frequently turns out to be singularly at variance with reality. For some reason or other, I had idly dreamed of Saratoga as buried in a sort of elegant wilderness of verdurous gloom. I fancied a region of shady forest drives, with a bright, broad-piazzaed hotel gleaming here and there against a background of mysterious groves and glades. I had made a cruelly small allowance for the stern vulgarities of life—for the shops and sidewalks and loafers, the complex machinery of a city of pleasure. The fault was so wholly my own that it is quite without bitterness that I proceed to affirm that the Saratoga of experience is sadly different from this. I confess, however, that it has always seemed to me that one's visions, on the whole, gain more than they lose by realization. There is an essential indignity in indefiniteness: you cannot imagine the especial poignant interest of details and accidents. They give more to the imagination than they receive from it. I frankly admit, therefore, that I find here a decidedly more satisfactory sort of place than the all-too-primitive Elysium of my wanton fancy. It is indeed, as I say, immensely different. There is a vast number of brick—nay, of asphalte—sidewalks, a great many shops, and a magnificent array of loafers. But what indeed are you to do at Saratoga—the morning draught having been achieved—unless you loaf? *"Que faire en un gîte à moins que l'on ne songe?"* Loafers being assumed, of course shops and sidewalks follow. The main avenue of Saratoga is in fact bravely entitled Broadway. The un-travelled reader may form a very accurate idea of it by recalling as distinctly as possible, not indeed the splendors of that famous thoroughfare, but the secondary charms of the Sixth Avenue. The place has what the French would call the "accent" of the Sixth Avenue. Its two main features are the two monster hotels which stand facing each other along a goodly portion of its course.

One, I believe, is considered much better than the other—less prodigious and promiscuous and tumultuous, but in appearance there is little choice between them. Both are immense brick structures, directly on the crowded, noisy street, with vast covered piazzas running along the façade, supported by great iron posts. The piazza of the Union Hotel, I have been repeatedly informed, is the largest "in the world." There are a number of objects in Saratoga, by the way, which in their respective kinds are the finest in the world. One of these is Mr. John Morrissey's casino. I bowed my head submissively to this statement, but privately I thought of the blue Mediterranean, and the little white promontory of Monaco, and the silver-gray verdure of olives, and the view across the outer sea toward the bosky cliffs of Italy. Congress Spring, too, it is well known, is the most delicious mineral spring in the known universe; this I am perfectly willing to maintain.

The piazzas of these great hotels may very well be the greatest of all piazzas. They are not picturesque, but they doubtless serve their purpose—that of affording sitting-space in the open air to an immense number of persons. They are, of course, quite the best places to observe the Saratoga world. In the evening, when the "boarders" have all come forth and seated themselves in groups, or have begun to stroll in (not always, I regret to say, to the sad detriment of the dramatic interest, bisexual) couples, the vast heterogeneous scene affords a great deal of entertainment. Seeing it for the first time, the observer is likely to assure himself

3

that he has neglected an important feature in the sum of American manners. The rough brick wall of the house, illumined by a line of flaring gas-lights, forms a harmonious background to the crude, impermanent, discordant tone of the assembly. In the larger of the two hotels, a series of long windows open into an immense parlor—the largest, I suppose, in the world—and the most scantily furnished, I imagine, in proportion to its size. A few dozen rocking-chairs, an equal number of small tables, tripods to the eternal ice-pitchers, serve chiefly to emphasize the vacuous grandeur of the spot. On the piazza, in the outer multitude, ladies largely prevail, both by numbers and (you are not slow to perceive) by distinction of appearance. The good old times of Saratoga, I believe, as of the world in general, are rapidly passing away. The time was when it was the chosen resort of none but "nice people." At the present day, I hear it constantly affirmed, "the company is dreadfully mixed." What society may have been at Saratoga when its elements were thus simple and severe, I can only vaguely, regretfully conjecture. I confine myself to the dense, democratic, vulgar Saratoga of the current year. You are struck, to begin with, at the hotels by the numerical superiority of the women; then, I think, by their personal superiority. It is incontestably the case that in appearance, in manner, in grace and completeness of aspect, American women vastly surpass their husbands and brothers. The case is reversed with most of the nations of Europe—with the English notably, and in some

4

degree with the French and Germans. Attached to the main entrance of the Union Hotel, and adjoining the ascent from the street to the piazza, is a "stoop" of mighty area, which, at most hours of the day and morning, is a favored lounging-place of men. I am one of those who think that on the whole we are a decidedly good-looking people. "On the whole," perhaps, every people is good-looking. There is, however, a type of physiognomy among ourselves which seems so potently to imperil the modest validity of this dictum, that one finally utters it with a certain sense of triumph. The lean, sallow, angular Yankee of tradition is dignified mainly by a look of decision, a hint of unimpassioned volition, the air of "smartness." This in some degree redeems him, but it fails to make him handsome. But in the average American of the present time, the typical leanness and sallowness are less, and the individual keenness and smartness at once equally intense and more evenly balanced with this greater comeliness of form. Casting your eye over a group of your fellow-citizens in the portico of the Union Hotel, you will be inclined to admit that, taking the good with the bad, they are worthy sons of the great Republic. I find in them, I confess, an ample fund of grave entertainment. They suggest to my fancy the swarming vastness—the multifarious possibilities and activities—of our young civilization. They come from the uttermost ends of the continent—from San Francisco, from New Orleans, from Duluth. As they sit with their white hats tilted forward, and their chairs tilted back, and their feet tilted up, and their cigars and tooth-picks forming various angles with these various lines, I imagine them surrounded with a sort of clear achromatic halo of mystery. They are obviously persons of experience—of a somewhat narrow and monotonous experience certainly; an experience of which the diamonds and laces which their wives are exhibiting hard by are, perhaps, the most substantial and beautiful result; but, at any rate, they are men who have positively actually lived. For the time, they are lounging with the negro waiters, and the boot-blacks, and the news-venders; but it was not in lounging that they gained their hard wrinkles and the level impartial regard which they direct from beneath their hat-rims. They are not the mellow fruit of a society impelled by tradition and attended by culture; they are hard nuts, which have grown and ripened as they could. When they talk among themselves, I seem to hear the mutual cracking of opposed shells.

If these men are remarkable, the ladies are wonderful. Saratoga is famous, I believe, as the place of all places in America where women most adorn themselves, or as the place, at least, where the greatest amount of dressing may be seen by the greatest number of people. Your first impression is therefore of the—what shall I call it?—of the *muchness* of the feminine drapery. Every woman you meet, young or old, is attired with a certain amount of splendor and a large amount of good taste. You behold an interesting, indeed a quite momentous spectacle: the democratization of elegance. If I am to believe what I hear—in fact, I may say what I overhear—a large portion of these sumptuous persons are victims of imperfect education and members of a somewhat narrow social circle. She walks more or less of a queen, however, each unsanctified nobody. She has, in dress, an admirable instinct of elegance and even of what the French call "chic." This instinct occasionally amounts to a sort of passion; the result then is superb. You look at the coarse brick walls, the rusty iron posts of the piazza, at the shuffling negro waiters, the great tawdry steamboat cabin of a drawing-room—you see the tilted ill-dressed loungers on the steps—and you finally regret that a figure so exquisite should have so vulgar a setting. Your resentment, however, is speedily tempered by reflection. You feel the impertinence of your old reminiscences of Old-World novels, and of the dreary social order in which privacy was the presiding genius and women arrayed themselves for the appreciation of the few—the few still, even when numerous. The crowd, the tavern loungers, the surrounding ugliness and tumult and license, constitute the social medium of the young lady whom you so cunningly admire: she is dressed for publicity. The thought fills you with a kind of awe. The Old-World social order is far away indeed, and as for Old-World novels, you begin to doubt whether she is so amiably curious as to read even the silliest of them. To be so excessively dressed is obviously to give pledges to idleness. I have been forcibly struck with the apparent absence of any warmth and richness of detail in the lives of these wonderful ladies of the piazzas. We are freely accused of being an eminently wasteful people: I know of few things which so largely warrant the accusation as the fact that these consummate élégantes adorn themselves, socially speaking, to so little purpose. To dress for every one is, practically, to dress for no one. There are few prettier sights than a charmingly dressed woman, gracefully established in some shady spot, with a piece of needlework or embroidery, or a book. Nothing very serious is accomplished, probably, but an aesthetic principle is considered. The embroidery and the book are a tribute to culture, and I suppose they really figure somewhere out of the opening scenes of French comedies. But here at Saratoga, at any hour of morning or evening, you may see a hundred brave creatures steeped in a quite unutterable empty handedness. I have had constant observation of a lady who seems to me really to possess a genius for being nothing more than dressed. Her dresses are admirably rich and beautiful—my letter would greatly gain in value if I possessed the learning needful for describing them. I can only say that every evening for a fortnight, I believe, she has revealed herself as a fresh creation. But she especially, as I say, has struck me as a person dressed beyond her life. I resent on her behalf—or on behalf at least of her finery—the extreme severity of her circumstances. What is she, after all, but a regular boarder? She ought to sit on the terrace of a stately castle, with a great baronial park shutting out the undressed world, mildly coquet-

8

ting with an ambassador or a duke. My imagination is shocked when I behold her seated in gorgeous relief against the dusty clapboards of the hotel, with her beautiful hands folded in her silken lap, her head drooping slightly beneath the weight of her *chignon*, her lips parted in a vague contemplative gaze at Mr. Helmbold's well-known advertisement on the opposite fence, her husband beside her reading the New York *Sun*.

I have indeed observed cases of a sort of splendid social isolation here, which are not without a certain amount of pathos—people who know no one—who have money and finery and possessions, only no friends. Such at least is my inference, from the lonely grandeur with which I see them invested. Women, of course, are the most helpless victims of this cruel situation, although it must be said that they befriend each other with a generosity for which we hardly give them credit. I have seen women, for instance, at various "hops," approach their lonely sisters and invite them to waltz, and I have seen the fair invited most graciously heedless of the potential irony of this particular form of charity. Gentlemen at Saratoga are at a premium far more, evidently, than at European watering-places. It is an old story that in this country we have no leisured class—the class from which the Saratogas of Europe recruit a large number of their male frequenters. A few months ago, I paid a visit to a famous English watering-place, where, among many substantial points of difference from our own, I chiefly remember the goodly number of well-dressed, well-looking, well-talking young men. While their sweethearts and sisters are waltzing together, our own young men are rolling up greenbacks in counting-houses and stores. I was recently reminded in another way, one evening, of the unlikeness of Saratoga to Cheltenham. Behind the biggest of the big hotels is a large planted yard, which has come to be talked of as a "park." This I regret, inasmuch as, as a yard, it is possibly the biggest in the world; while as a park I am afraid it is decidedly less than the smallest. At one end, however, stands a great ball-room, approached by a range of wooden steps. It was late in the evening: the room, in spite of the intense heat, was blazing with light, and the orchestra thundering a mighty waltz. A group of loungers, including myself, were hanging about to watch the ingress of the festally minded. In the basement of the edifice, sunk beneath the ground, a noisy auctioneer, in his shirt and trousers, black in the face with heat and vociferation, was selling "pools" of the races to a dense group of frowsy betting-men. At the foot of the steps was stationed a man in a linen coat and straw hat, without waistcoat or cravat, to take the tickets of the ball-goers. As the latter failed to arrive in sufficient numbers, a musician came forth to the top of the steps and blew a loud summons on a horn. After this they began to straggle along. On this occasion, certainly, the company promised to be decidedly "mixed." The women, as usual, were a great deal dressed, though without any constant adhesion to the technicalities of full-dress. The men adhered to it neither in the letter nor the spirit. The possessor of a pair of satin shod feet, twinkling beneath an uplifted volume of gauze and lace and flowers, tripped up the steps with her gloved hand on the sleeve of a railway "duster." Now and then two ladies arrived alone: generally a group of them approached under convoy of a single man. Children were freely scattered among their elders, and frequently a small boy would deliver his ticket and enter the glittering portal, beautifully unembarrassed. Of the children of Saratoga there would be wondrous things to relate. I believe that, in spite of their valuable aid, the festival of which I speak was rated rather a "fizzle." I see it advertised that they are soon to have, for their own peculiar benefit, a "Masquerade and Promenade Concert, beginning at 9 p.m." I observe that they usually open the "hops," and that it is only after their elders have borrowed confidence from the sight of their unfaltering paces that they venture to perform. You meet them far into the evening roaming over the piazzas and corridors of the hotels—the little girls especially—lean, pale, and formidable. Occasionally childhood confesses itself, even when motherhood stands out, and you see at eleven o'clock at night some poor little bedizened precocity collapsed in slumbers in a lonely wayside chair. The part played by children in society here is only an additional instance of the wholesale equalization of the various social atoms which is the distinctive feature of collective Saratoga: A man in a "duster" at a ball is as good as a man in irreproachable sable; a young woman dancing with another young woman is as good as a young woman dancing with a young man; a child of ten is as good as a woman of thirty; a double negative in conversation is rather better than a single.

An important feature in many watering-places is the facility for leaving it a little behind you and tasting of the unmitigated country. You may wander to some shady hillside and sentimentalize upon the vanity of high civilization. But at Saratoga civilization holds you fast. The most important feature of the place, perhaps, is the impossibility of realizing any such pastoral dream. The surrounding country is a charming wilderness, but the roads are so abominably bad that walking and driving are alike unprofitable. Of course, however, if you are bent upon a walk, you will take it. There is a striking contrast between the concentrated prodigality of life in the immediate precinct of the hotels and the generous wooded wildness and roughness into which half an hour's stroll may lead you. Only a mile behind you are thousands of loungers and idlers, fashioned from head to foot by the experience of cities and keenly knowing in their secrets; while here, about you and before you, blooms untamed the hardy innocence of field and forest. The heavy roads are little more than sandy wheel-tracks; by the tangled wayside the blackberries wither unpicked. The country undulates with a beautiful unsoftened freedom. There are no white villages gleaming in the distance, no spires of churches, no salient details. It is all green, lonely, and vacant. If you wish to seize an "effect," you must stop beneath a cluster of pines and listen to the murmur of the softly-troubled air, or follow upward the gradual bending of their trunks to where the afternoon light touches and enchants them. Here and there on a slope by the roadside stands a rough unpainted farm-house, looking as if its dreary blackness were the result of its standing dark and lonely amid so many months, and such a wide expanse, of winter snow. The principal feature of the grassy un-furnished yard is the great wood-pile, telling grimly of the long reversion of the summer. For the time, however, it looks down contentedly enough over a goodly appanage of grain-fields and orchards, and I can fancy that it may be good to be a boy there. But to be a man, it must be quite what the lean, brown, serious farmers physiognomically hint it to be. You have, however, at the present season, for your additional beguilement, on the east-ern horizon, the vision of the long bold chain of the Green Mountains, clad in that single coat of simple candid blue which is the favorite garment of our American hills. As a visitor, too, you have for an afternoon's excursion your choice between a couple of lakes. Saratoga Lake, the larger and more distant of the two, is the goal of the regular afternoon drive. Above the shore is a well-appointed tavern—"Moon's" it is called by the voice of fame—where you may sit upon a broad piazza and par-take of fried potatoes and "drinks"; the latter, if you happen to have come from poor dislicensed Boston, a peculiarly gratifying privilege. You enjoy the felicity sighed for by that wanton Italian princess of the anecdote, when, one summer evening, to the sound of music, she wished that to eat an ice were a sin. The other lake is small, and its shores are unadorned by any edifice but a boat-house, where you may hire a skiff and pull yourself out into the minnow-tickled, wood-circled oval. Here, floating in its darkened half, while you watch on the opposite shore the tree-stems, white and sharp in the declining sunlight, and their foliage whitening and whispering in the breeze, and you feel that this little solitude is part of a greater and more portentous solitude, you may resolve certain passages of Ruskin, in which he dwells upon the needfulness of some human association, however remote, to make natural scenery fully impressive. You may recall that magnificent passage in which he relates having tried with such fatal effect, in a battle-haunted valley of the Jura, to fancy himself in a nameless solitude of our own continent. You feel around you, with irresistible force, the serene inexperience of undedicated nature—the absence of serious associations, the nearness, indeed, of the vulgar and trivial associations of the least picturesque of great watering-places—you feel this, and you wonder what it is you so deeply and calmly enjoy. You conclude, possibly, that it is a great advantage to be able at once to enjoy Ruskin and to enjoy what Ruskin dispraises. And hereupon you return to your hotel and read the New York papers on the plan of the French campaign and the Twenty-third Street murder.

LAKE GEORGE
August 10, 1870

Lake George, ca. 1873.

I FIND SO GREAT A PLEASURE IN TRAVELLING, AND MAINTAIN so friendly and expectant an attitude toward possible "sensations," that they haven't the heart to leave me altogether unvisited, though I confess that they are frequently such as may seem to lack flavor to fastidious people or to those sated with many wanderings. I found it a sensation, for instance, to come from Saratoga (for the first time) in a "drawing-room car." I found it a luxury of an almost romantic intensity to sit in one of those revolving *fauteuils* and gaze through that generous, oblong plate of glass at the midsummer wilderness which bordered my route, while through a nether screen of delicate wire the summer breeze rushed in, winnowed of the grossness of cinders, and an artfully frescoed ceiling invited my gaze to rest at moments from the excessive *abandon* of nature. I observed that my companions on top of the coach which I subsequently mounted, were unanimous in voting Glenn's Falls a remarkably pretty town: I therefore observed it with the view at once of enjoying its prettiness and of appraising my neighbor's judgment. Pretty it is for a town of elements so meagre. Like Saratoga, the village is blissfully bedimmed and over-shadowed with a noble abundance of wayside verdure—by serried lines of elms and maples, and their goodly domestic umbrage in gardens and yards. It has not, however, that rounded and harmonious charm which would perhaps have made it appear a little less incongruous to me than it did to behold a public work of art at our egress from the village. Like so many other little American towns, it has its own little aesthetic fact—shining with newness—in the shape of a soldier's monument: an obelisk, if I recollect, of a pleasant cream-colored stone, surmounted on its apex by a species of napkin, which an eagle is in the act of rending in his claws, and decorated toward the bases with four niches, enclosing four of the usual warriors contemplating the graves of their comrades. It is not very wisely conceived, perhaps, nor very cunningly executed; but there it stands, neighbored by a grosser ugliness, which, in its fair monumental breadth and permanence, it may connect with some

lurking germs of future beauty. The drive to Lake George is full
of a grand rough prettiness—leading you straight into the midst
of the thickening hills and along the bases of half-grown mountains. When you emerge upon the lake, you find yourself fairly
launched into the romance of mountain scenery.

I find here, at this little village of Caldwell, an immense hotel of a good deal of external architectural pretension—French-
roofed, with a sort of high-piled and gabled complexity which,
as country hotels go, makes it look vaguely picturesque. It stands
directly on the lake, and boasts a really magnificent piazza—a
terrace of contemplation—worthy of the beautiful view it commands. This, I believe, is not the choice quarter of the lake. Yet
such as it is, it is thoroughly lovely. Great simple masses of
wooded hills rise with a plain green nearness, to right and left;
further, as the lake recedes, they increase in size and in magic of
colors, and in the uttermost background they figure nobly in
outline and hue, with the magnitude and mystery of a mountain
chain. A friend at Saratoga informed me that Lake George is
considered strongly to resemble the Lake of Como. A year ago,
almost at the present moment, I spent a week on the shores of
that divinest of lakes, and I think that, even unreminded by my
friends, I should occasionally be prompted to an attempt at
comparison and contrast. It is in a certain way unwise and even
unkind to play this sort of game with the things of America and
of Italy, but it seems to me that comparisons are odious only

when they are sterile, and intruders only when they are forced. Lake George is quite enough like the Lake of Como to impel you, if the image of the latter is fresh in your mind, to pursue the likeness to its inevitable phase of unlikeness. The mountains which melt into those blue Italian waters are clad with olives and vines, with groves of mulberry and chestnut and ilex, with a verdure productive of a wholly different range of effects from that of the sombre forests of the North. And yet, such is the infinite mercy of the sun, its inscrutable cunning and power, that, to-day, as the morning light spent itself through the long hours over the sullen darkness of these American hills, it tempered and tinted and softened them, and wrought upon them such a sweet confusion of exquisite tones, such a dimness of distant blue, such a brilliant tissue of noonday vapors, such a fine-drawn purity of outline, that they seemed to borrow their beauty from a Southern air and to shine with that mild, iridescent, opaline glow which you enjoy from the little headland above Bellagio. It is the complete absence of detail which betrays the identity of American scenery. On those Italian slopes the fancy travels with the eye from one bright sign of human presence to another, from a gleaming mountain hamlet to the lonely twinkle of a mountain shrine. In our own landscape, if the background in its greatest beauty is in a sense common, undetermined, and general, the foreground is even more so, inasmuch as in the foreground there is usually an attempt at detail. Here, on the left shore of the lake, is a saw-mill with a high black chimney, a dozen little white wooden houses, and a little promontory of planks on posts, in the nature of a steamboat-pier. This brave little attempt at civilization looks as transient and accidental as the furniture of a dream. Above it mounts the long-drawn roundness of the wooded hills. Their woods of course supply the saw-mill, and the saw-mill supplies the excellent plank-road. I followed this road yesterday through the village to a point where, having entered the relapsing woods, it throws out two tributary arms. The plank-road pursues its way to other little settlements, expectant of the coach. One of the other roads keeps along the lake—"a little piece away," as a young girl of the country told me. The third observes a middling course, along the lower slope of the hills, above the lake road. I wandered along the last, to excellent purpose as regards the pursuit of the picturesque: through the coolness of thinly divided woods, past little bald grey farm-houses, lonely and sunny in their midsummer plenitude, past an occasional cottage of gentility—a built and dedicated point of view. I shall long remember a certain little farm-house before which I stayed my steps to stare and enjoy. If the pure picturesque means simply the presentation of a picture, self-informed and complete, I have seen nothing in Italy or England which better deserves the praise. Here, for once, the picture swarmed with detail—less, however, with the scattered accessories of the usual warm-toned farmstead of tradition than with the rich invasive presence of spontaneous nature and the tangled overgrowth of rank vegetation. No Tuscan *podere* could have been more densely and gracefully luxuriant. The little unpainted dwelling stood on a grassy slope—leaden-grey in the shade, silver-grey in the sun. Against the darkness of the open doorway, from where I stood, I saw a white butterfly soar and sink—I almost heard in the noonday stillness the soundless whirr of his wings. The milk-pans glittered in the sun; beside the house-wall a magnificent clump of pink hollyhocks lifted its blooming stalks, touching almost the roof, and adding the hint of another color to the abounding green and yellow and blue. The deeper grass, toward the fence and roadside, was a great expansive blaze of golden-rod. It seemed to glitter upward toward the milder yellow of the crowded apples in the crowded trees of the orchard. This orchard—its trees all high and noble in spite of their bended breadth—lost itself in a tangled confusion of verdurous background, so that it was hard to say whether it was an orchard run wild with excessive productiveness, or a piece of the mountain wilderness come down to be tame and prolific. At any rate, I have seldom seen a more potent emanation of reflected composite light and color, of leafed and bladed and fruited green.

I made my way down a sloping lane to the road which adheres to the lake and thence by a path across a wooded field to the verge of the water. Here I wandered along the narrow strip of beach to a little sandy cove, and lay down with my head in the shade of a thicket of bushes. The pebbles lay unstirred at my feet; the water was sheeted with the noonday light; the opposite mountains were clothed with wonderful tones of atmospheric blue. I tried to study them, to distinguish them, to remember them; but I felt only that they were wonderful, and that they don't belong to the province of words. The mountains at all hours have a way of trying to put off the observer with a certain *faux air* of simplicity: a single great curve for an outline, a dozen alternate planes of deeper or fainter blue for its contents. The persistent observer very soon learns, however, what to make of this brave simplicity—or rather, he very soon learns how hard it is to make anything positive of it, to resolve it into its thousand magical parts. It is an old story that the mountains are for ever changing, that they live and move in a series of shifting and melting and amazing "effects"; but I never so deeply felt its meaning as while I lay on that couch of unrolled pebbles and gazed at them across that shining-level which assures the freedom of the interval of air. The clouds were stationed in a windless volume just above the line of their summits. Above the empty lake was an empty field of sky. The result, of course, on the slopes of the hills was a series of exquisite operations in light—doubly fine and delicate from the stillness of the air. The general tone was immensely soft and luminous—so that, as I say, I might very well have been on the Lake of Como or on

Lago Maggiore. A green island lay blooming in the middle of the lake—which was not the Isola Bella, but apparently a plain small thicket of firs. The oars of a little boat twinkled in the sun and wrinkled the waveless deep. I chased the great slow shadows on the mountains into little shadows, and the little shadows into shadows which still were great. I followed the even blue into violet and pink and amber. I disintegrated with a steady gaze the long pure sky-lines into linked miles of innumerable lonely spires. And then at last I rose to my feet feeling that I had learned chiefly to misreport these mountain wonders.

In the late afternoon, I went upon the lake lazily, with a red-necked, brawn-eyed young rustic as an oarsman. It was, of course, delicious. The closing day had drained the water of its early glare and dyed it with cool blue shadows. The hotel, from the lake, looked decidedly vulgar. The mountains, in the gross richness of their deepening blue, made at last an approach to a large massive simplicity. It is not till the sun departs, I think, that you see them in their essential masses. The aerial charm is gone, but they gain in formal grandeur. In the evening, at the hotel, there was the usual array of placid, sauntering tourists— the usual spectacle of high-heeled young ladies in those charming puffed and panniered overdresses of white muslin which are now so picturesquely worn. I confess, however, that to myself the most interesting feature of the evening was the band of musicians on the piazza. The New York papers had just come in, and I had been reading of the great deeds of Prussia and the confusion of France. I was filled with a sense of Prussian greatness. Strolling toward the place where the band was stationed, I beheld behind every trumpet a sturdy German face and heard in every note an uplifted German voice. My sense of German greatness was hugely magnified. Here, while their strong fellow-citizens were winning battles and making history in Alsace and Lorraine, they were making music in a distant land for a crowd of unmelodious strangers. What a splendid range of prowess and powers! What an omen for the Prussian future! The air seemed a brazen paean of triumph and joy. Their simple Teutonic presence seemed a portent.

FROM LAKE GEORGE
TO BURLINGTON

August 12, 1870

Lake Champlain, New York.

I HAVE SPENT TO-DAY AMID LAKES AND MOUNTAINS. I LEFT the further end of Lake George in a little steamer in the early morning. The three hours' sail which you thus obtain is full of delightful beauty. The whole lake is framed in the noblest, purest mountain-masses. On the sides of the mountains, as we started, the clouds lay heavy and low, shutting us in, almost, to our little world of water; and during our transit they occasionally broke into rapid momentary rain; but on the whole I think they gave us quite as many effects as they concealed. At moments, when they thinned and lifted, the pale watery light yellowed the heavy darkness of the ranged forests into a languid counterfeit of autumn. The circling mountains faded and deepened in this passage like arriving and departing ghosts. The great hills group themselves about the upper portions of Lake George with a multitudinous majesty and variety which I shall not attempt to describe. They recede in dimly vaporous bays, where you barely feel their grim walls darkening through the cold gray sheets of cloud; they protrude in great headlands and break the mist with their cliffed and crested foreheads. The especial beauty of Lake George is believed to consist in its innumerable little islands. Many of these are extremely small—a growing-place for a dozen trees; several are large enough to contain a couple of houses. On one of them we saw some brave pleasure-seekers encamped, who came down to the water's edge in the rain and cheered us with a beautiful, cheerful bravado. The scenery about the lake, as a whole, is such a vast simple undisturbed wilderness, that you are almost startled to behold these various little makeshifts of civilization; you half wonder at our capital little steamer and at the young ladies from the hotel on the deck, with copies of "Lothair" in their hands. Landing at the head of the lake, we mounted on stages and drove some four miles to Ticonderoga and the edge of Lake Champlain—passing on our way through a little village which seemed to me, save for its setting of hills, more drearily, dirtily, glaringly void of any poor, pitiful little incident of village prettiness than a village with as fine a name—it was called Ticonderoga—had a right to be. The last mile of the four brings you into a bit of country prettier to my eye, almost, than any other in all this beautiful region. Through a poor wooden gateway, erected as if with a sort of sense of its guarded treasure, you enter a great tract of grassy slopes and scattered trees, which seem to tell you that nature herself has determined for once to aim at pure privacy, and to bestow upon a great rough expanse of American woodland the distinction of aspect of a nobleman's park. The short grass rolls downward in easy slopes, shaded by dense yet desultory groups of walnut and oak. You glance down the short vistas, as if to discover a browsing deer, or, perhaps, in the purer essence of romance and of baronial landscape, the sauntering daughter of an earl. But the pleasant avenue brings you only to the simple ruins of the grass-grown fort and to a sudden view of Champlain at your feet.

Of the fort I shall not speak: I dined, perforce, in the halfhour during which I might fastingly have explored it. I saw it only from the top of the coach as we passed. It seemed to me in quite the perfection of decay—of stony decrepitude and verdurous overgrowth—and to exhale with sufficient force a meagre historic melancholy. I prefer to speak of the lake, though of this, indeed, there is but little to say, and I have little space to say it. My sail hitherward of four hours showed me the most and the best of it. There is something, to my sense, in the physiognomy of Lake Champlain delightfully free, noble, and open. It is narrow for a lake and broad for a river, yet it strikes you more as a river. The water is less blue and pure than that of Lake George—a concession of quality to quantity. But its great beauty is the really great style of the landscape: this grand unflowing river, as it seems, with the generous, prolonged simplicity of its shores—green and level, without being low, on the east (till you come abreast of the Green Mountains), on the west bordered by an immense panorama of magnificent hills, receding more dimly from line to line till they meet the steady azure of the great wall of the Adirondacks. At Burlington your seeming river broadens as if to the meeting of the sea, and the forward horizon becomes a long water-line. Hereabouts the Green Mountains rise up in the east to gaze across the broad interval at their marshalled peers in New York. The vast reach of the lake and this double mountain view go far to make Burlington a supremely beautiful town. I know of it only so much as I learned in an hour's stroll, after my arrival. The lower portion by the lake-side is savagely raw and shabby, but as it ascends the long hill, which it partly covers, it gradually becomes the most truly charming, I fancy, of New England country towns. I followed a long street which leaves the hotel, crosses a rough, shallow ravine, which seems to divide it from the ugly poorness of the commercial quarter, and ascends a stately, shaded, residential avenue to no less a pinnacle of dignity than the University of Vermont. The university is a plain red building, with a cupola of beaten tin, shining like the dome of a Greek church, modestly embowered in scholastic shade—shade as modest as the number of its last batch of graduates, which I wouldn't for the world repeat. It faces a small enclosed and planted common; the whole spot is full of civic greenness and stillness and sweetness. It pleased me deeply, considering what it was; it reminded me the least bit in the world of a sort of primitive development of an English cathedral close. On the summit of the hill, where it leaves the town, you embrace the whole circling presence of the distant mountains; you see Mount Mansfield looking over lake and land at Mount Marcy. Equally with the view, though—I had been having views all day—I enjoyed, as I passed again along the avenue, the pleasant, solid American homes, with their blooming breadth of garden, sacred with peace and summer and twilight. I say "solid" with intent; the most of them seemed to have been tested and ripened by time. One of them there was—but of it I shall say nothing. I reserve it for its proper immortality in the first chapter of the great American novel. It perhaps added a touch to my light impression of the old and the graceful that, as I wandered back to my hotel in the dusk, I heard repeatedly, as the home-faring laborers passed me in couples, the sound of a tongue of other than Yankee inflections. It was Canadian French.

NEWPORT
September 5, 1870

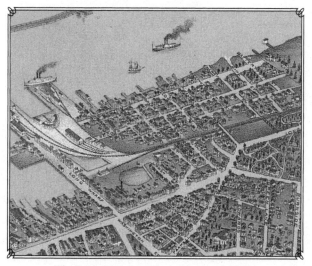

The Point, Newport, Rhode Island, ca. 1878.

THE SEASON AT NEWPORT HAS AN OBSTINATE LIFE. September has fairly begun, but as yet there is small visible diminution in the steady stream—the splendid, stupid stream—of carriages which rolls in the afternoon along the Avenue. There is, I think, a far more intimate fondness between Newport and its frequenters than that which in most American watering-places consecrates the somewhat mechanical relation between the visitors and the visited. This relation here is for the most part slightly sentimental. I am very far from professing a cynical contempt for the gaieties and vanities of Newport life: they are, as a spectacle, extremely amusing; they are full of a certain warmth of social color which charms alike the eye and the fancy; they are worth observing, if only to conclude against them; they possess at least the dignity of all extreme and emphatic expressions of a social tendency; but they are not so far from "*was uns alle bändigt, das Gemeine*" that I do not seem to overhear at times the still, small voice of this tender sense of the sweet, superior beauty of the local influences that surround them, pleading gently in their favor to the fastidious critic. I feel almost warranted in saying that here this exquisite natural background has sunk less in relative value and suffered less from the encroachments of pleasure-seeking man than the scenic properties of any other great watering-place. For this, perhaps, we may thank rather the modest, incorruptible integrity of the Newport landscape than any very intelligent forbearance on the part of the summer colony. The beauty of this landscape is so subtle, so essential, so humble, so much a thing of character and impression, so little a thing of feature and pretension, that it cunningly eludes the grasp of the destroyer or the reformer, and triumphs in impalpable purity even when it seems to condescend. I have sometimes wondered in sternly rational moods why it is that

Newport is so loved of the votaries of idleness and pleasure. Its resources are few in number. It is emphatically circumscribed. It has few drives, few walks, little variety of scenery. Its charms and its interest are confined to a narrow circle. It has of course the unlimited ocean, but seafaring idlers are of necessity the fortunate few. Last evening, it seemed to me, as I drove along the Avenue, that my wonderment was quenched for ever. The atmospheric tone, the exquisite, rich simplicity of the landscape, gave mild, enchanting sense of positive climate—these are the real charm of Newport, and the secret of her supremacy. You are melted by the admirable art of the landscape, by seeing so much that is lovely and impressive achieved with such a masterly frugality of means—with so little parade of the vast, the various, or the rare, with so narrow a range of color and form. I could not help thinking, as I turned from the great harmony of elegance and the unfathomable mystery of purity which lay deepening on the breast of nature with the various shades of twilight, to the motley discord and lavish wholesale splendor of the flowing stream of gentility on the Avenue, that, quite in their own line of effect, these money-made social heroes and heroines might learn a few good lessons from the daily prospect of the great western expanse of rock and ocean in its relations with the declining sun. But this is a rather fantastic demand. Many persons of course come to Newport simply because others come, and in this way the present brilliant colony has grown up. Let me not be suspected, when I speak of Newport, of the untasteful heresy of meaning primarily rocks and waves rather than ladies and gentlemen.

The ladies and gentlemen are in great force—the ladies, of course, especially. It is true everywhere, I suppose, that women are the central animating element of "society"; but you feel this to be especially true as you pass along the Newport Avenue. I doubt whether anywhere else women enjoy so largely what is called a "good time" with so small a sacrifice, that is, of the luxury of self-respect. I heard a lady yesterday tell another, with a quiet ecstasy of tone, that she had been having a "most perfect time." This is the very poetry of pleasure. In England, if our impression is correct, women hold the second fiddle in the great social harmony. You will never, at the sight of a carriage-load of mild-browed English maidens, with a presiding matron, plump and passive, in the midst of them, suspect their countrywomen of enjoying in the conventional world anything more than a fictitious and deputed dignity. They neither speak nor act from themselves, but from their husbands and brothers and lovers. On the Continent, women are proclaimed supreme; but we fancy them, with more or less justice, as maintaining their empire by various clandestine and reprehensible arts. With us—we may say it without bravado—they are both free and unsophisticated. You feel it most gratefully as you receive a confident bow from a pretty young girl in her basket-phaeton. She is very young

and very pretty, but she has a certain delicate breadth of movement which seems to you a pure gain, without imaginable taint
of loss. She combines, you reflect with respectful tenderness, the
utmost of modesty with the least possible shyness. Shyness is
certainly very pretty—when it is not very ugly; but shyness may
often darken the bloom of genuine modesty, and a certain feminine frankness and confidence may often incline it toward the
light. Let us assume, then, that all the young ladies whom you
may meet here are the correctest of all possible young ladies. In
the course of time, they ripen into the delightful women who
divide your admiration. It is easy to see that Newport must be a
most agreeable sojourn for the male sex. The gentlemen, indeed,
look wonderfully prosperous and well-conditioned. They gallop
on shining horses or recline in a sort of coaxing Herculean sub-
mission beside the lovely mistress of a phaeton. Young men—
and young old men—I have occasion to observe, are far more
numerous than at Saratoga, and of vastly superior quality. There
is, indeed, in all things a striking difference in tone and aspect
between these two great cities of pleasure. After Saratoga, Newport seems really substantial and civilized. Aesthetically speaking, you may remain at Newport with a fairly good conscience;
at Saratoga, you linger on under passionate protest. At Newport,
life is public, if you will; at Saratoga, it is absolutely common.
The difference, in a word, is the difference between a group of
three or four hotels and a series of cottages and villas. Saratoga

perhaps deserves our greater homage, as being characteristically democratic and American; let us, then, make Saratoga the heaven of our aspiration, but let us yet a while content ourselves with Newport as the lordly earth of our residence.

The villas and cottages, the beautiful idle women, the beautiful idle men, the brilliant pleasure-fraught days and evenings, impart, perhaps, to Newport life a faintly European expression, in so far as they suggest the somewhat alien presence of leisure— "fine old Leisure," as George Eliot calls it. Nothing, it seems to me, however, can take place in America without straightway seeming very American; and, after a week at Newport, you begin to fancy that, to live for amusement simply, beyond the noise of commerce or of care, is a distinctively national trait. Nowhere else in this country—nowhere, of course, within the range of our better civilization—does business seem so remote, so vague and unreal. Here a positive organic system of idleness or of active pleasure-taking has grown up and matured. If there is any poetry in the ignorance of trade and turmoil and the hard processes of fortune, Newport may claim her share of it. She knows—or at least appears to know—for the most part, nothing but results. Individuals here, of course, have private cares and burdens, to preserve the balance and the dignity of life; but these collective society conspires to forget. It is a singular fact that a society that does nothing is decidedly more picturesque, more interesting to the eye of sentiment, than a society which is

hard at work. Newport, in this way, is infinitely more picturesque than Saratoga. There you feel that idleness is occasional,
empirical. Most of the people you see are asking themselves, you
imagine, whether the game is worth the candle, and work is not
better than such toilsome play. But here, obviously, the habit of
pleasure is formed, and (within the limits of a generous morality) many of the secrets of pleasure are known. Do what we will,
on certain lines Europe is ahead of us yet. Newport falls altogether short of Baden-Baden in her presentment of the impro-
prieties. They are altogether absent from the picture, which is
therefore signally destitute of those shades of color produced by
the mysteries and fascinations of vice. But idleness *per se* is vicious, and of course you may imagine what you please. For my
own part, I prefer to imagine nothing but the graceful and the
pure; and, with the help of such imaginings, you may construct
a very pretty sentimental counterpart to the superficial movement of society. This I lately found very difficult to do at Saratoga. Sentiment there is pitifully shy and elusive. Here, the
multiplied relations of men and women, under the permanent
pressure of luxury and idleness, give it a very fair chance. Sentiment, indeed, of masterly force and interest, springs up in every
soil, with a sovereign disregard of occasion. People love and
hate and aspire with the greatest intensity when they have to
make their time and privilege. I should hardly come to Newport
for the materials of a tragedy. Even in their own kind, the social

elements are as yet too light and thin. But I can fancy finding here the plot of many a pleasant sentimental comedy. I can almost imagine, indeed, a transient observer of the Newport spectacle dreaming momentarily of a great American novel, in which the heroine shall be infinitely realistic, and yet neither a schoolmistress nor an outcast. I say intentionally the "transient" observer, because I fancy that here the suspicion only is friendly to dramatic peace; the knowledge is hostile. The observer would discover, on a nearer view, I rather fear, that his possible heroines have too unexceptionally a perpetual "good time."

This will remind the reader of what he must already have heard affirmed, that to speak of a place with abundance you must know it, but not too well. I feel as if I knew the natural elements of Newport too well to attempt to describe them. I have known them so long that I hardly know what I think of them. I have little more than a simple consciousness of vastly enjoying them. Even this consciousness at times lies dumb and inert. I wonder at such times whether, to appeal fairly to the general human sense, the prospect here has not something too much of the extra-terrestrial element. Life seems too short, space too narrow, to warrant you in giving in an unqualified adhesion to a *paysage* which is two-thirds ocean. For the most part, however, I am willing to take the landscape as it stands, and to think that, without its native complement of sea, the land would lose much of its beauty. It is, in fact, a land exquisitely modified by marine influences. Indeed, in spite of all the evil it has done me, I could find it in my soul to love the sea when I consider how it co-operates with the Newport promontories to the delight of the eye. Give it up altogether, and you can thus enjoy it still, reflected and immobilized—like the Prussian army a month hence.

Newport consists, as the reader will know, of an ancient and honorable town, a goodly harbor, and a long, broad neck of land, stretching southward into the sea, and forming the chief habitation of the summer colony. Along the greater part of its eastward length, this projecting coast is bordered with lordly cliffs and dotted with seaward-gazing villas. At the head of the promontory the villas enjoy a magnificent reach of prospect. The pure Atlantic—the Old World westward tides—expire directly at their feet. Behind the line of villas runs the Avenue, with more villas yet—of which there is nothing at all to say, but that those built recently are a hundred times prettier than those built fifteen years ago, offering a modest contribution to our modern architectural Renaissance. Some years ago, when I first knew Newport, the town proper was considered extremely "picturesque." If an antique shabbiness that amounts almost to squalor is a pertinent element, as I believe it is, of the picturesque, the little main street at least—Thames Street by name—still deserves the praise. Here, in their crooked and dwarfish wooden mansions, are the shops that minister to the daily needs of the expanded city; and here of a summer morning, jolting over the cobble-stones of the narrow roadway, you may see a hundred superfine ladies seeking with languid eagerness what they may buy—to "buy something," I believe, being a diurnal necessity of the American woman of substance. This busy region gradually melts away into the grass-grown stillness of the Point, in the eyes of many persons the pleasantest quarter in Newport. It has superficially the advantage of being as yet uninvaded by fashion. When I first knew it, however, its peculiar charm was even more undisturbed than at present. The Point may be called the old residential, as distinguished from the commercial, town. It is meagre, shallow, and scanty—a mere pinch of antiquity—but, as far as it goes, it retains an exquisite tone. It leaves the shops and the little wharves, and wanders close to the harbor, where the breeze-borne rattle of shifted sails and spars alone intrudes upon its stillness, till its mouldy-timbered quiet subsides into the low, tame rocks and beaches which edge the bay. Several fine modern houses have recently been erected on the water-side, absorbing the sober, primitive tenements which used to maintain the picturesque character of the place. They improve it, of course, as a residence, but they injure it as a spectacle. Enough of early architecture still remains, however, to suggest a multitude of thoughts as to the severe simplicity of the generation which produced it. It is picturesque in a way, but with a paucity of elements which seems to defy all effect. The plain gray nudity of these little warped and shingled boxes seems utterly to repudiate the slightest curiosity. But here, as elsewhere, the magical Newport atmosphere wins half the battle. It aims at no mystery. It clothes them in a garment of absolute light. Their homely notches and splinters twinkle in the sun. Their steep gray roofs, barnacled with lichens, remind you of old scows, overturned on the beach to dry. They show for what they are—simple houses by the sea. Over-darkened by no wealth of inland shade, without show or elegance or finish, they patiently partake of the fortunes of the era—of the vast blue glare which rises from the bay, and the storms which sweep inward from the ocean. They have been blown free of all needless accretion of detail—scorched clean of all graceful superfluities. Most of the population of this part of Newport is, I believe, of Quaker lineage. This double-salted Quakerism is abundant motive for this soundless and colorless simplicity.

One of the more recent movements of fashion is the so-called "New Drive"—the beautiful drive by the sea. The Avenue, where the Neck abruptly terminates, has been made to prolong itself to the west, and to wander for a couple of miles over a lovely region of beach and lowly down and sandy meadow and salt brown sheep-grass. This region was formerly the most beautiful part of Newport—the least frequented and the most untamed by fashion. I by no means regret the creation of the new road, however. A walker may very soon isolate himself, and the occupants of carriages stand a chance of benefit quite superior to their power of injury. The peculiar charm of this great westward expanse is very difficult to define. It is in an especial degree the charm of Newport in general—the combined lowness of tone, as painters call it, in all the earthy elements, and the extraordinary elevation of tone in the air. For miles and miles you see at your feet, in mingled shades of yellow and gray, a desolate waste of moss-clad rock and sand-starved grass. At your left surges and shines the mighty presence of the vast immediate sea. Above the broken and composite level of this double-featured plain, the great heavens ascend in innumerable stages of light. In spite of the bare simplicity of this prospect, its beauty is far more a beauty of detail than that of the average American landscape. Descend into a hollow of the rocks, into one of the little warm climates of five feet square which you may find there, beside the grateful ocean glare, and you will be struck quite as much by their fineness as by their roughness. From time to time, as you wander, you will meet a lonely, stunted tree, into the storm-twisted multiplicity of whose branches all the possible grace and grotesqueness of the growth of trees seem to have been finely concentrated. The region of which I speak is perhaps best seen in the late afternoon, from the high seat of a carriage on the Avenue. You seem to stand just without the threshold of the west. At its opposite extremity sinks the sun, with such a splendor, perhaps, as I lately saw—a splendor of the deepest blue, more luminous and fiery than the fiercest of our common vespertinal crimsons, all streaked and barred with blown and drifted gold. The whole vast interval, with its rocks and marshes and ponds, seems bedimmed into a troubled monotone of glorious purple. The near Atlantic is fading slowly into the unborrowed darkness of its deep, essential life. In the foreground, a short distance from the road, an old orchard uplifts its tangled stems and branches against the violet mists of the west. It seems strangely grotesque and enchanted. No ancient olive grove of Italy or Provence was ever more hoarily romantic. This is what people commonly behold on the last homeward bend of the drive. For such of them as are happy enough to occupy one of the villas on the cliffs, the beauty of the day has even yet not expired. The present summer has been emphatically the summer of moonlights. Not the nights, however, but the long days, in these agreeable homes, are what specially appeal to my fancy. Here you find a solution of the insoluble problem—to combine an abundance of society with an abundance of solitude. In their charming broad-windowed drawing-rooms, on their great seaward piazzas, within sight of the serious Atlantic horizon, which is so familiar to the eye and so mysterious to the heart, caressed by the gentle breeze which makes all but simple, social, delightful *then* and *there* seem unreal and untasteful—the sweet fruit of the lotus grows more than ever succulent and magical. You feel here not more a man, perhaps, but more a passive gentleman and worldling.

How sensible they ought to be, the denizens of these pleasant places, of their peculiar felicity and distinction! How it should purify their tempers and refine their intellects! How delicate, how wise, how discriminating they should become! What excellent manners and fancies their situation should generate! How it should purge them of vulgarity! Happy *villeggianti* of Newport!

NIAGARA

September 28, 1871

American Falls from Goat Island,
Niagara, New York.

I.

My journey hitherward by a morning's sail from Toronto across Lake Ontario, seemed to me, as regards a certain dull vacuity in this episode of travel, a kind of calculated preparation for the uproar of Niagara—a pause or hush on the threshold of a great sensation; and this, too, in spite of the reverent attention I was mindful to bestow on the first-seen, in my experience, of the great lakes. It has the merit, from the shore, of producing a slight perplexity of vision. It is the sea, and yet just not the sea. The huge expanse, the landless line of the horizon, suggest the ocean; while an indefinable shortness of pulse, a kind of fresh-water gentleness of tone, seem to contradict the idea. What meets the eye is on the ocean scale, but you feel somehow that the lake is a thing of smaller spirit. Lake navigation, therefore, seems to me not especially entertaining. The scene tends to of-fer, as one may say, a sort of marine-effect *manqué*. It has the blankness and vacancy of the sea without that vast essential swell which, amid the belting brine, so often saves the situation to the eye. I was occupied, as we crossed, in wondering whether this dull reduction of the ocean contained that which could properly be termed "scenery." At the mouth of the Niagara River, however, after a three hours' sail, scenery really begins, and very soon crowds upon you in force. The steamer puts into the narrow channel of the stream, and heads upward between high embankments. From this point, I think, you really enter into relations with Niagara. Little by little the elements become a picture, rich with the shadows of coming events. You have a foretaste of the great spectacle of color which you enjoy at the Falls. The even cliffs of red-brown earth are now crusted, now spotted, with autumnal orange and crimson, and laden with this ardent boskage plunge sheer into the deep-dyed green of the river. As you proceed, the river begins to tell its tale—at first in broken syllables of foam and flurry, and then, as it were, in rushing, flashing sentences and passionate interjections. Onwards from Lewiston, where you are transferred from the boat to the train, you see it from the cope of the American cliff, far beneath you, now superbly unnavigable. You have a lively sense of something happening ahead; the river, as a man near me said, has evidently been in a row. The cliffs here are immense; they form genuine *vomitoria* worthy of the living floods whose exit they protect. This is the first act of the drama of Niagara; for it is, I believe, one of the commonplaces of description that you instinctively harmonize and dramatize it. At the station pertaining to the railway suspension-bridge, you see in mid-air beyond an interval of murky confusion produced by the further bridge, the smoke of the trains, and the thickened atmosphere of the peopled bank, a huge far-flashing sheet which glares through the distance as a monstrous absorbent and irradiant of light. And here, in the interest of the picturesque, let me note that this obstructive bridge tends in a way to enhance the first glimpse of the cataract. Its long black span, falling dead along the shining brow of the Falls, seems shivered and smitten by their fierce effulgence, and trembles across the field of vision like some mighty mote in an excess of light. A moment later, as the train proceeds, you plunge into the village, and the cataract, save as a vague ground-tone to this trivial interlude, is, like so many other goals of aesthetic pilgrimage, temporarily postponed to the hotel.

With this postponement comes, I think, an immediate decline of expectation; for there is every appearance that the spectacle you have come so far to see is to be choked in the horribly vulgar shops and booths and catchpenny artifices which have pushed and elbowed to within the very spray of the Falls, and ply their importunities in shrill competition with its thunder. You see a multitude of hotels and taverns and shops, glaring with white paint, bedizened with placards and advertisements, and decorated by groups of those gentlemen who flourish most rankly on the soil of New York and in the vicinage of hotels; who carry their hands in their pockets, wear their hats always and every way, and, although of a sedentary habit, yet spurn the earth with their heels. A side-glimpse of the Falls, however, calls out one's philosophy; you reflect that this is but such a sordid foreground as Turner liked to use; you hurry to where the roar grows louder, and, I was going to say, you escape from the village. In fact, however, you don't escape from it; it is constantly at your elbow, just to the right or the left of the line of contemplation. It would be paying Niagara a poor compliment to say that, practically, she does not hurl off this chaffering by-play from her cope; but as you value the integrity of your impression, you are bound to affirm that it hereby suffers appreciable abatement. You wonder, as you stroll about, whether it is altogether an unrighteous dream that with the slow progress of culture, and the possible or impossible growth of some larger comprehension of beauty and fitness, the public conscience may not tend to ensure to such sovereign phases of nature something of the inviolability and privacy which we are slow to bestow, indeed, upon fame, but which we do not grudge at least to art. We place a great picture, a great statue, in a museum; we erect a great monument in the centre of our largest square, and if we can suppose ourselves nowadays building a cathedral, we should certainly isolate it as much as possible and subject it to no ignoble contact. We cannot build about Niagara with walls and a roof, nor girdle it with a palisade, but the sentimental tourist may muse upon the chances of its being guarded by the negative homage of empty spaces and absent barracks and decent forbearance. The actual abuse of the scene belongs evidently to that immense class of iniquities which are destined to grow very much worse in order to grow a very little better. The good humor engendered by the main spectacle bids you suffer it to run its course.

Though hereabouts so much is great, distances are small, and a ramble of two or three hours enables you to gaze hither and thither from a dozen standpoints. The one you are likely to choose first is that on the Canada cliff, something above the suspension bridge. The great fall faces you, enshrined in the surging increase of its own resounding mists. The common feeling just here, I believe, is one of disappointment at its want of height; the vision grasps less in quantity than it had been prompted to expect. My own sense, I confess, was absolutely gratified from the first; and, indeed, not the bulk and volume of the matter, but its exquisite *expression*, seemed to me paramount. You are, moreover, at some distance, and you feel that with the lessening interval you will not be cheated of your chance to be dizzied with pure size. Already you see the world-famous green, baffling painters, baffling poets, clear and lucid on the lip of the precipice; the more so, of course, for the clouds of silver and snow into which it drops transformed. The whole picture before you is admirably simple. The Horseshoe gleams and glares and boils and smokes from the centre to the right, drumming itself dim with vapors; in the centre, the dark pedestal of Goat Island divides the double flood; to the left booms and smokes the minor thunder of the American Fall; and, on a level with the eye, above the still crest of either cataract, appear the white faces of the uttermost rapids. The circle of weltering froth at the base of the Horseshoe, emerging from the dead white vapors—absolute white, as moonless midnight is absolute black—which muffle impenetrably the final crash of the plunge, melts slowly into the powerful green of the lower river. It seems a mighty drama in itself, this blanched survival and recovery of the stream. It stretches away like a tired swimmer, struggling from the snowy scum and the silver drift, and passing slowly from an eddying foam-sheet, touched with green lights, to a cold stony green, streaked and marbled with trails and wild arabesques of foam. This is the beginning of that air of unforgotten trouble which marks the river as you meet it at the lake. The ultimate green I speak of is of admirable hue—the clearest, the greenest, the coldest of all greens—a green as sombre and steady as most greens are light and inconstant. So it shifts along, with a sort of measured pride, deep and lucid, and yet of immense *body*, the most stately, the least turbid of torrents. Its movement, its sweep, and progression are as admirable as its color, but as little as its color to be made a matter of words. These things are but part of a spectacle in which nothing is imperfect. As you draw nearer and nearer, on the Canada cliff, to the right arm of the Horseshoe, the mass begins in all conscience to be large enough. You are able at last to stand on the very cope of the shelf from which the leap is taken, bathing your boot-toes, if you like, in the side-ooze of the glassy curve. I may say, in parenthesis, that the importunities one suffers here, amid the central din of the cataract, from hackmen and photographers and venders of gimcracks, are simply hideous and infamous. The road is lined with little drinking-shops and warehouses, and from these retreats their occupants dart forth in competition upon the hapless traveller with talk of their pigmy sideshows. I can but ask—*need* such things be? You purchase release at last by a great outlay of the small coin of dogged "No's," and stand steeped in long looks at the most beautiful object in the world.

II.

The pure beauty of elegance and grace is the grand characteristic of the Fall. It is not in the least monstrous. It is supremely artistic—a harmony, a conception, a masterpiece; it beats Michael Angelo. One may seem at first to say the least, but the delicate observer will admit that one says the most, in saying that it is *pleasing*. There are, however, so many more things to say about it—its multitudinous features crowd so upon the vision as one looks—that it seems absurd for me to attempt to handle details. The main feature, perhaps, is the incomparable loveliness of the immense line of the river and its lateral abutments. It neither falters, nor breaks, nor stiffens, but maintains grandly from wing to wing its consummate curve. This noble line is worthily sustained by mighty pillars of alternate emerald and marble. The famous green loses nothing, as you may imagine, on a nearer view. A green more gorgeously cool and pure it is impossible to conceive. It is to the vulgar greens of earth what the blue of a summer sky is to our mundane azures, and is, in fact, as sacred, as remote, as impalpable as that. You can fancy it the parent-green, the head-spring of color to all the verdant water-caves and all the clear, sub-fluvial haunts and bowers of naiads and mermen in all the streams of the earth. The lower half of the watery wall is shrouded in the steam of the boiling gulf—a veil never rent nor lifted. At its core, this eternal cloud seems fixed and still with excess of motion—still and intensely white; but, as it rolls and climbs against its lucent cliff, it tosses little whiffs and fumes and pants of snowy smoke, which betray the furious tumult of its dazzling womb. In the middle of the curve, at the apex of the gulf, the converging walls are ground into finest powder, and hence arises a huge mist-column, and fills the upper air with its hovering drift. Its summit far overtops the crest of the cataract, and, as you look down along the rapids above, you see it hanging over the averted gulf like some far-flowing ensign of danger. Of these things some vulgar verbal hint may be attempted; but what words can render the rarest charm of all—the clear-cut brow of the Fall, the very act and figure of the leap, the rounded turn of the horizontal to the perpendicular? To call it simple seems a florid over-statement. Anything less combined and complicated never appealed to the admiration of men. It is carved clean as an emerald, as one must say and say again. It arrives, it pauses, it plunges; it comes and goes for ever; it melts and shifts and changes, all with the sound as of a thousand thunderbolts; and yet its pure outline never lapses by a bubble's value from its constant calm. It is as gentle as the pouring of wine from a flagon—of melody from the lip of a singer. From the little grove beside the American Fall you catch superbly—better than you are able to do at the Horseshoe—the very profile of this full-flooded bend. If the line of beauty had vanished from the earth elsewhere, it would survive on this classic forehead. It is impossible to insist too strongly on the prodigious *elegance* of the great Fall, as seen from the Canada cliff. You fancy that the genius who contrived it was verily the prime author of the truth that order, measure, and symmetry are the conditions of perfect beauty. He applied his faith among the watching and listening forests, long before the Greeks proclaimed theirs in the shining masonry of the Acropolis. Rage, confusion, chaos, are grandly absent; dignity, grace, and leisure ride upon the crest; it flows without haste, without rest, with the measured majesty of a motion whose rhythm is attuned to eternity. Even the roll of the white batteries at the base seems fixed and poised and ordered, and in the vague middle zone of difference between falling flood and rising cloud you imagine a mystical meaning—the passage of body to soul, of matter to spirit, of human to divine.

Goat Island, of which every one has heard, is the great menagerie of lions, and the spot where your single stone—or, in plain prose, your half-dollar—kills most birds. This broad insular strip, which performs the excellent office of withholding the American shore from immediate contact with the Fall, has been allowed to remain a very proper piece of wildness, and here you may ramble, for the most part, in undiverted contemplation. The island is owned, I believe, by a family of co-heritors, who have the good taste to preserve it intact. More than once, however, as I have been told, they have been offered a huge price for the privilege of building a hotel upon this sacred soil. They have been wise, but, after all, they are human, and the offer may be made once too often. Before this fatal day dawns, why shouldn't the State buy up the precious acres, as California has done the Yo-Semite? It is the opinion of a sentimental tourist that no price would be too great to pay. Otherwise, the only hope for their integrity is in the possibility of a shrewd prevision on the part of the gentlemen who know how to keep hotels that the music of the dinner-band would be injured by the roar of the cataract. You approach from Goat Island the left abutment of the Horseshoe. The little tower which, with the classic rainbow, figures in all "views" of the scene, is planted at a dozen feet from the shore, directly on the shoulder of the Fall. This little tower, I think, deserves a compliment. One might have said beforehand that it would never do, but, as it stands, it is incontestably picturesque. It serves as a unit of appreciation of the scale of things, and from its spray-blackened summit it admits you to an almost downward peep into the green gulf. More here, even, than on the Canada edge, you perceive how the great spectacle is wrought all in water. Its substantial floods take on at moments the likeness of walls and pillars and columns, and, to present any vivid picture of them, we are compelled to talk freely of emerald and crystal, of silver and marble. But really, all the simplicity of the Falls, and half their grandeur, reside in the fact that they are built clean of fluid elements, and that no rocky staging or earthy commixture avail to complicate and vulgarize them. They are water piled on water, pinned on water, hinging and hanging on water, breaking, crashing, whitening in mutual masses of water. And yet for all this no solid was ever solid like that sculptured shoulder of the Horseshoe! From this little tower, or, better still, from various points further along the island-shore, it seems indeed a watery world. Before you stretches the huge expanse of the upper river, with its belittled cliffs, now mere black lines of forest, dull as with the sadness of gazing at eternal storm. Anything more horribly desolate than this boundless livid welter of the rapids it is impossible to conceive, and you very soon begin to pay it the tribute of your terror, in the impulse to people it with human forms. On this theme you can spin endless romances. Yes, they are alive, every fear-blanched billow and eddy of them—alive and frenzied with the sense of their doom. They see below them that nameless pause of the arrested current, and the high-tossed drift of sound and spray which rises up lamenting, like the ghosts of their murdered brothers. They shriek, they sob, they clasp their white hands and toss their long hair; they cling and clutch and wrestle, and, above all, they *bite*. Especially tragical is the air they have of being forced backward, with averted faces, to their fate. Every portion of the flood is like the grim stride of a giant, wading huge-kneed to his purpose, with the white teeth of a victim fastened in his neck. The outermost of three small islands, interconnected by short bridges, at the extremity of this shore, places one in singularly intimate relation with this portentous flurry. To say that hereabouts the water leaps and plunges and rears and dives, that its uproar deadens the thunder, and its swiftness distances the lightning, is to say all that we can, and yet but a tithe of what we should. Nowhere surely in the wide world is water handled with such a masterly knowledge of effect.

The great spectacle may be called complete only when you have gone down the river some four miles, on the American side, to the so-called rapids of the Whirlpool. Here the unhappy stream tremendously renews its trouble. Two approaches have been contrived on the cliff—one to the rapids proper, the other, further below, to the scene of the sudden bend. The first consists of a little wooden cage, of the "elevator" pattern, which slides up and down a gigantic perpendicular shaft of horrible flimsiness. But a couple of the usual little brides, staggering beneath the weight of gorgeous cashmeres, entered the conveyance with their respective consorts at the same time with myself; and, as it thus carried Hymen and his fortunes, we survived the adventure. You obtain from below—that is, on the shore of the river—a specimen of as noble cliff-scenery as the continent can afford. The green embankment at the base of the sheer red wall is by itself a very fair mountain-slope; and from this starts erect, rugged and raw, a grandly spacious lateral section of mother earth. As it stands, Gustave Doré might have drawn it. He would have sketched with especial ardor certain parasitical shrubs and boskages—lone and dizzy witnesses of autumn; certain outward-peering wens and warts and other perpendicular excrescences of rock; and, above all, near the summit, the fantastic figures of sundry audacious minor cliffs, grafted upon the greater by a mere lateral attachment and based in the empty air, with great lone trees rooted on their verges, like the tower of the Palazzo Vecchio at Florence. The actual whirlpool is a third of a mile further down the river, and is best seen from the cliff above. Thus seen, it seems to me by all odds the finest of the secondary episodes of the Niagara drama, and one on which a scribbling tourist, ineffectively playing at showman, may be content to ring down his curtain. The channel at this point turns away to the right, at a clean right-angle, and the river, arriving from the rapids just above with stupendous velocity, meets the hollow elbow of the Canada shore. The movement with which it betrays its surprise and bewilderment—the sudden issueless maze of waters—is, I think, after the Horseshoe Fall, the superbest thing in its progress. It breaks into no small rage; the offending cliffs receive no drop of spray; for the flood moves in a body and wastes no vulgar side-spurts; but you see it shaken to its innermost bowels and panting hugely, as if smothered in its excessive volume. Pressed back upon its centre, the current creates a sort of pivot, from which it eddies, groping for exit in vast slow circles, barely outlined in foam. The Canada shore, shaggy and gaudy with late

September foliage, closes about it like the rising shelves of an amphitheatre, and deepens by contrast the strong blue-green of the stream. This slow-revolving basin resembles nothing so much as some ancient palace-pavement, cracked and scratched by the butts of legionary spears and the gold stiffened hem of the garments of kings.

A EUROPEAN SUMMER:
LICHFIELD AND WARWICK

June 11, 1872

*The Samuel Johnson statue in Lichfield,
with the artist, 1859.*

To write at Oxford of anything but Oxford requires, on the part of the sentimental tourist, no small power of mental abstraction. Yet I have it at heart to pay to three or four other scenes recently visited the debt of an enjoyment hardly less profound than my relish for this scholastic paradise. First

among these is the cathedral city of Lichfield. I say the city, because Lichfield has a character of its own apart from its great
ecclesiastical feature. In the centre of its little market-place—
dullest and sleepiest of provincial market-places—rises a huge
effigy of Dr. Johnson, the *genius loci*, who was constructed, hu-
manly, with very nearly as large an architecture as the great
abbey. The doctor's statue, which is of some plaster-like compound, painted a shiny brown, and of no great merit of design,
fills out the vacant dulness of the little square in much the same
way as his massive personality occupies—with just a margin for
Garrick—the record of his native town. In one of the volumes
of Croker's "Boswell" is a steel plate of the old Johnsonian birth-
house, by the aid of a vague recollection of which I detected the
dwelling beneath its modernized frontage. It bears no mural inscription, and, save for a hint of antiquity in the receding basement, with pillars supporting the floor above, seems in no
especial harmony with Johnson's time or fame. Lichfield in general appeared to me, indeed, to have little to say about her great
son, beyond the fact that the dreary provincial quality of the
local atmosphere, in which it is so easy to fancy a great intellectual appetite turning sick with inanition, may help to explain
the doctor's subsequent, almost ferocious, fondness for London.
I walked about the silent streets, trying to repeople them with
wigs and short clothes, and, while I lingered near the cathedral,
endeavored to guess the message of its Gothic graces to John-

son's ponderous classicism. But I achieved but a colorless picture at the best, and the most vivid image in my mind's eye was that of the London Coach facing towards Temple Bar, with the young author of "Rasselas" scowling nearsightedly from the cheapest seat. With him goes the interest of Lichfield town. The place is stale, without being really antique. It is as if that prodigious temperament had absorbed and appropriated its original vitality.

If every dull provincial town, however, formed but a girdle of quietude to a cathedral as rich as that of Lichfield, one would thank it for its unimportunate vacancy. Lichfield Cathedral is great among churches, and bravely performs the prime duty of a cathedral—that of seeming for the time (to minds unsophisticated by architectural culture) the finest, on the whole, of all cathedrals. This one is rather oddly placed, on the slope of a hill, the particular spot having been chosen, I believe, because sanctified by the sufferings of certain primitive martyrs; but it is fine to see how its upper portions surmount any crookedness of posture, and its great towers overtake in mid-air the conditions of perfect symmetry.

The close is a singularly pleasant one. A long sheet of water expands behind it, and, besides leading the eye off into a sweet green landscape, renders the inestimable service of reflecting the three spires as they rise above the great trees which mask the Palace and the Deanery. These august abodes cope the northern side of the slope, and stand back behind huge gateposts and close-wrought gates which seem to enclose a sort of Georgian atmosphere. Before them stretches a row of huge elms, which must have been old when Johnson was young; and between these and the long-buttressed wall of the cathedral, you may stroll to and fro among as pleasant a mixture of influences (I imagine) as any in England. You can stand back here, too, from the west front further than in many cases, and examine at your ease its lavish decoration. You are, perhaps, a trifle too much at your ease; for you soon discover what a more cursory glance might not betray, that the immense façade has been covered with stucco and paint, that an effigy of Charles II, in wig and plumes and trunk-hose, of almost Gothic grotesqueness, surmounts the middle window; that the various other statues of saints and kings have but recently climbed into their niches; and that the whole expanse, in short, is a *pastiche*. All this was done some fifty years ago, in the taste of that day as to restoration, and yet it but partially mitigates the impressiveness of the high façade, with its brace of spires, and the great embossed and image-fretted surface, to which the lowness of the portals (the too frequent reproach of English abbeys) seems to give a loftier reach. Passing beneath one of these low portals, however, I found myself gazing down as noble a church vista as any I remember. The Cathedral is of magnificent length, and the screen between nave and choir has been removed, so that from stem to

stern, as we may say, of the great vessel of the church, it is all a
mighty avenue of multitudinous slender columns, terminating in
what seems a great screen of ruby and sapphire and topaz—one
of the finest east windows in England. The Cathedral is narrow
in proportion to its length; it is the long-drawn aisle of the poet
in perfection, and there is something grandly elegant in the
unity of effect produced by this undiverted perspective. The
charm is increased by a singular architectural phantasy. Standing in the centre of the doorway, you perceive that the eastern
wall does not directly face you, and that from the beginning of
the choir the receding aisle deflects slightly to the left—in suggestion of the droop of the Saviour's head on the cross. Here, as
elsewhere, Mr. Gilbert Scott has recently been at work—to excellent purpose, from what the sacristan related of the barbarous
encroachments of the last century. This extraordinary period expended an incalculable amount of imagination in proving that it
had none. Universal whitewash was the least of its offences. But
this has been scraped away, and the solid stonework left to speak
for itself—the delicate capitals and cornices disencrusted and
discreetly rechiselled, and the whole temple aesthetically reded-
icated. Its most beautiful feature, happily, has needed no repair,
for its perfect beauty has been its safeguard. The great choir window of Lichfield is the noblest glass-work I remember to have
seen. I have met nowhere colors so chaste and grave, and yet so
rich and true, nor a cluster of designs so piously decorative, and

yet so pictorial. Such a window as this seems to me the most sacred ornament of a great church—to be, not like vault and screen and altar, the dim contingent promise of heaven, but the very assurance and presence of it. This Lichfield glass is not the less interesting for being visibly of foreign origin. Exceeding so obviously as it does the range of English genius in this line, it indicates at least the heavenly treasure stored up in continental churches. It dates from the early sixteenth century, and was transferred hither sixty years ago from the suppressed abbey of Heckenroode, in Belgium. This, however, is not all of Lichfield. You have not seen it till you have strolled and restrolled along the close on every side, and watched the three spires constantly change their relation as you move and pause. Nothing can well be finer than the combination of the two lesser ones soaring equally in front, and the third riding tremendously the magnificently sustained line of the roof. At a certain distance against the sky, this long ridge seems something infinite, and the great spire to sit astride of it like a giant mounted on a mastodon. Your sense of the huge mass of the building is deepened by the fact that though the central steeple is of double the elevation of the others, you see it, from some points, borne back in a perspective which drops it to half their stature, and lifts them into immensity. But it would take long to tell all that one sees and fancies and thinks in a lingering walk about so great a church as this. There are few deeper pleasures than such a contemplative stroll.

To walk in quest of any object that one has more or less tenderly dreamed of—to find your way—to steal upon it softly—to see at last, if it is church or castle, the tower-tops peeping above elms or beeches—to push forward with a rush, and emerge, and pause, and draw that first long breath which is the compromise between so many sensations—this is a pleasure left to the tourist even after the broad glare of photography has dissipated so many of the sweet mysteries of travel—even in a season when he is fatally apt to meet a dozen fellow-pilgrims returning from the shrine, each *gros Jean comme devant*, or to overtake a dozen more, telegraphing their impressions down the line as they arrive. Such a pleasure I lately enjoyed, quite in its perfection, in a walk to Haddon Hall, along a meadow-path by the Wye, in this interminable English twilight, which I am never weary of admiring, watch in hand. Haddon Hall lies among Derbyshire hills, in a region infested, I was about to write, by Americans. But I achieved my own sly pilgrimage in perfect solitude; and as I descried the gray walls among the rook-haunted elms, I felt not like a tourist, but like an adventurer. I have certainly had, as a tourist, few more charming moments than some—such as any one, I suppose, is free to have—that I passed on a little ruined gray bridge which spans, with its single narrow arch, a trickling stream at the base of the eminence from which those walls and trees look down. The twilight deepened, the ragged battlements and the low, broad oriels glanced duskily from the foliage, the rooks wheeled and clamored in the glowing sky, and if there had been a ghost on the premises, I certainly ought to have seen it. In fact, I did see it, as we see ghosts nowadays. I felt the incommunicable spirit of the scene with almost painful intensity. The old life, the old manners, the old figures seemed present again. The great *coup de théâtre* of the young woman who shows you the Hall—it is rather languidly done on her part—is to point out a little dusky door opening from a turret to a back terrace as the aperture through which Dorothy Vernon eloped with Lord John Manners. I was ignorant of this episode, for I was not to enter the Hall till the morrow; and I am still unversed in the history of the actors. But as I stood in the luminous dusk weaving the romance of the spot, I divined Dorothy Vernon, and felt very much like a Lord John. It was, of course, on just such an evening that the delicious event came off, and, by listening with the proper credulity, I might surely hear on the flags of the castle-court the ghostly foot-fall of a daughter of the race. The only footfall I can conscientiously swear to, however, is the by no means ghostly tread of the damsel who led me through the mansion in the prosier light of the next morning. Haddon Hall, I believe, is one of the places in which it is the fashion to be "disappointed"; a fact explained in a great measure by the absence of a formal approach to the house, which shows its low, gray front to every trudger on the high-road. But the charm of the place is so much less that of grandeur than that of melancholy, that it is rather deepened than diminished by this attitude of obvious survival and decay. And for that matter, when you have entered the steep little outer court through the huge thickness of the low gateway, the present seems effectually walled out, and the past walled in—like a dead man in a sepulchre. It is very dead, of a fine June morning, the genius of Haddon Hall; and the silent courts and chambers, with their hues of ashen gray and faded brown, seem as time-bleached as the dry bones of any mouldering organism. The comparison is odd; but Haddon Hall reminded me perversely of some of the larger houses at Pompeii. The private life of the past is revealed in each case with very much the same distinctness and on a small enough scale not to stagger the imagination. This old dwelling, indeed, has so little of the mass and expanse of the classic feudal castle that it almost suggests one of those miniature models of great buildings which lurk in dusty corners of museums. But it is large enough to be deliciously complete and to contain an infinite store of the poetry of grass-grown courts looked into by long, low oriel casements, and climbed out of by crooked stone stairways, mounting against the walls to little high-placed doors. The "tone" of Haddon Hall, of all its walls and towers and stonework, is the gray of unpolished silver, and the reader who has been in England need hardly be reminded of the sweet accord—to eye and mind alike—existing between all stony surfaces covered with the real white rust of time and the deep living green of the strong ivy which seems to feed on their slow decay. Of this effect and of a hundred others—from those that belong to low-browed, stone-paved empty rooms, where countesses used to trail their cloth-of-gold over rushes, to those one may note where the dark tower stairway emerges at last, on a level with the highest beech-tops, against the cracked and sun-baked parapet, which flaunted the castle standard over the castle walls—of every form of sad desuetude and picturesque decay Haddon Hall contains some delightful examples. Its finish point is undoubtedly a certain court from which a stately flight of steps ascends to the terrace where that daughter of the Vernons whom I have mentioned proved that it was useless to have baptized her so primly. These steps, with the terrace, its balustrade topped with great ivy-muffled knobs of stone, and its vast background of lordly beeches, form the ideal *mise en scène* for portions of Shakespeare's comedies. "It's Elizabethan," said my companion. Here the Countess Olivia may have listened to the fantastic Malvolio, or Beatrix, superbest of flirts, have come to summon Benedick to dinner.

The glories of Chatsworth, which lies but a few miles from Haddon, serve as a fine *repoussoir* to its more delicate merits, just as they are supposed to gain, I believe, in the tourist's eyes, by contrast with its charming, its almost Italian shabbiness. But the glories of Chatsworth, incontestable as they are, were so effectually eclipsed to my mind, a couple of days later, that in future, when I think of an English mansion, I shall think only of Warwick, and when I think of an English park, only of Blenheim. Your run by train through the gentle Warwickshire landscape does much to prepare you for the great spectacle of the castle, which seems hardly more than a sort of massive symbol and synthesis of the broad prosperity and peace and leisure diffused over this great pastoral expanse. The Warwickshire meadows are to common English scenery what this is to that of the rest of the world. For mile upon mile you can see nothing but broad sloping pastures of velvet turf, overbrowsed by sheep of the most fantastic shagging, and ornamented with hedges out of the trailing luxury of whose verdure, great ivy-tangled oaks and elms arise with a kind of architectural regularity. The landscape, indeed, sins by excess of nutritive suggestion; it savors of the larder; it is too ovine, too bovine, too succulent, and if you were to believe what you see before you, this rugged globe would be a sort of boneless ball, neatly covered with some such plush-like integument as might be figured by the down on the cheek of a peach. But a great thought keeps you company as you go and gives character to the scenery. Warwickshire was Shakespeare's country. Those who think that a great genius is something supremely ripe and healthy, and human, may find comfort in the fact. It helps materially to complete my own vague conception of Shakespeare's temperament, with which I find it no great shock to be obliged to associate ideas of mutton and beef. There is something as final, as disillusioned of the romantic horrors of rock and forest, as deeply attuned to human needs, in the Warwickshire pastures, as there is in the underlying morality of the poet.

With human needs in general, Warwick Castle may be in no great accord, but few places are more gratifying to the sentimental tourist. It is the only great residence that I ever coveted as a home. The fire that we heard so much of last winter in America appears to have consumed but an inconsiderable and easily-spared portion of the house, and the great towers rise over the great trees and the town with the same grand air as before. Picturesquely, Warwick gains from not being sequestered, after the common fashion, in acres of park. The village-street winds about the garden walls, though its hum expires before it has had time to scale them. There can be no better example of the way in which stone-walls, if they do not of necessity make a prison, may on occasions make a palace, than the tremendous privacy maintained thus about a mansion whose windows and towers form the main feature of a bustling town. At Warwick the past joins hands so stoutly with the present that you can hardly say where one begins and the other ends, and you rather miss the various crannies and gaps of what I just now called the Italian shabbiness of Haddon. There is a Caesar's tower and a Guy's tower and half a dozen more, but they are so well-conditioned in their ponderous antiquity that you are at loss whether to consider them parts of an old house revived or of a new house picturesquely superannuated. Such as they are, however, plunging into the grassed and gravelled courts from which their battlements look really feudal, and into gardens large enough for all delight and too small, as they should be, to be amazing; and with ranges between them of great apartments at whose hugely recessed windows you may turn from Van Dyke and Rembrandt, to glance down the cliff-like pile into the Avon, washing the base like a lordly moat, with its bridge, and its trees, and its memories—they mark the very model of a great hereditary dwelling—one which amply satisfies the imagination without irritating the conscience. The pictures at Warwick reminded me afresh of an old conclusion on this matter, that the best fortune for good pictures is not to be crowded into public collections—not even into the relative privacy of *Salons carrés* and Tribunes, but to hang in largely-spaced half-dozens on the walls of fine houses. Here the historical atmosphere, as one may call it, is almost a compensation for the often imperfect light. If this is true of most pictures, it is especially so of the works of Van Dyke, whom you think of, wherever you may find him, as having, with that immense good-breeding which is the stamp of his manner, taken account in his painting of the local conditions, and predestined his picture to just the spot where it hangs. This is, in fact, an illusion as regards the Van Dykes at Warwick, for none of them represent members of the house. The very finest, perhaps, after the great melancholy, picturesque Charles I.—death, or at least the presentiment of death on the pale horse—is a portrait from the Brignole palace at Genoa, a beautiful noble matron in black, with her little son and heir. The last Van Dykes I had seen were the noble company this lady had left behind her in the Genoese palace, and as I looked at her, I thought of her mighty change of circumstance. Here she sits in the mild light of Midmost England; there you could almost fancy her blinking in the great glare sent up from the Mediterranean. Picturesque for picturesque, I should hardly know which to choose.

A EUROPEAN SUMMER:
NORTH DEVON
July 1872

Illsborough, Ilfracombe, England, ca. 1890.

FOR THOSE FANCIFUL OBSERVERS TO WHOM BROAD ENGLAND means chiefly the perfection of the rural picturesque, Devonshire means the perfection of England. I, at least, had so complacently taken it for granted that all the characteristic graces of English scenery are here to be found in especial exuberance that before we fairly crossed the borders I had begun to look impatiently from the carriage window for the veritable landscape in watercolors. Devonshire meets you promptly in all its purity. In the course of ten minutes you have been able to glance down the green vista of a dozen Devonshire lanes. On huge embankments of moss and turf, smothered in wild-flowers and embroidered with the finest lace-work of trailing ground-ivy, rise solid walls of flowering thorn and glistening holly and golden broom, and more strong, homely shrubs than I can name, and toss their blooming tangle to a sky which seems to look down between them in places from but a dozen inches of blue. They are over-strewn with lovely little flowers with names as delicate as their petals of gold and silver and azure—bird's-eye and ring's-finger and wandering-sailor—and their soil, a superb dark red, turns in spots so nearly to crimson that you almost fancy it some fantastic compound purchased at the chemist's and scattered there for ornament. The mingled reflection of this rich-hued earth and the dim green light which filters through the hedge, forms an effect to challenge the skill of the most accomplished water-colorist. A Devonshire cottage is no less striking a local "institution." Crushed beneath its burden of thatch, coated with a rough white stucco, of a tone to delight a painter, nestling in deep foliage, and garnished at doorstep and wayside with various forms of chubby infancy, it seems to have been stationed there for no more obvious purpose than to keep a promise to your fancy, though it covers, I suppose, not a little of the sordid misery which the fancy loves to forget. I rolled past lanes and cottages to Exeter, where I found a cathedral. When one has fairly tasted of the pleasure of cathedral-hunting, the approach to each new shrine gives a peculiarly agreeable zest to one's curiosity. You are making a collection of great impressions, and I think the process is in no case so delightful as applied to cathedrals. Going from one fine picture to another is certainly good, but the fine pictures of the world are terribly numerous, and they have a troublesome way of crowding and jostling each other in the memory. The number of cathedrals is small, and the mass and presence of each specimen is great, so that, as they rise in the mind in individual majesty, they dwarf all common impressions. They form, indeed, but a gallery of vaster pictures; for, when time has dulled the recollection of details, you retain a single broad image of the vast gray edifice, with its towers, its tone of color, and its still, green precinct. All this is especially true, perhaps, of one's memory of English cathedrals, which are almost alone in possessing, as pictures, the setting of a spacious and harmonious Close. The Cathedral stands supreme, but the Close makes the *scene*. Exeter is not one of the grandest, but, in common with great and small, it has certain points on which local learning expatiates with peculiar pride. Exeter, indeed, does itself injustice by a low, dark front, which not only diminishes the apparent altitude of the nave, but conceals, as you look eastward, two noble Norman towers. The front, however, which has a gloomy picturesqueness, is redeemed by two fine features: a magnificent rose-window, whose vast stone ribs (enclosing some very pallid last-century glass) are disposed with the most charming intricacy; and a long sculptured screen—a sort of stony band of images—which traverses the façade from side to side. The little broken-visaged effigies of saints and kings and bishops niched in tiers along this hoary wall are prodigiously black and quaint and primitive in expression, and as you look at them with whatever contemplative tenderness your trade of hard-working tourist may have left at your disposal, you fancy that somehow they are consciously historical—sensitive victims of time; that they feel the loss of their noses, their toes, and their crowns; and that, when the long June twilight turns at last to a deeper gray, and the quiet of the Close to a deeper stillness, they begin to peer sidewise out of their narrow recesses, and to converse in some strange form of early English, as rigid, yet as candid, as their features and postures, moaning, like a company of ancient paupers round a hospital fire, over their aches and infirmities and losses, and the sadness of being so terribly old. The vast square transeptal towers of the church seem to me to have the same sort of *personal* melancholy. Nothing in all architecture expresses better, to my imagination, the sadness of survival, the resignation of dogged material continuance, than a broad expanse of Norman stonework, roughly adorned with its low relief of short columns, and round arches, and almost barbarous hatchet-work, and lifted high into that mild English light which accords so well with its dull-gray surface. The especial secret of the impressiveness of such a Norman tower I cannot pretend to have discovered; it lies largely in the look of having been proudly and sturdily built—as if the masons had been urged by a trumpet-blast, and the stones squared by a battle-axe—contrasted with this mere idleness of antiquity and passive lapse into quaintness. A Greek temple preserves a kind of fresh immortality in its concentrated refinement, and a Gothic cathedral in its adventurous exuberance; but a Norman tower stands up like some simple strong man in his might, bending a melancholy brow upon an age which demands that strength shall be cunning.

The North Devon coast, whither it was my design on coming to Exeter to proceed, has the primary merit of being, as yet, virgin soil as to railways. I went accordingly from Barnstaple to Ilfracombe on the top of a coach, in the fashion of elder days; and, thanks to my position, I managed to enjoy the landscape in spite of the two worthy Englishmen before me who were reading aloud together, with a natural glee which might have passed for fiendish malice, the *Daily Telegraph's* painfully vivid account of the defeat of the *Atalanta* crew. It seemed to me, I remember, a sort of pledge and token of the invincibility of English muscle that a newspaper record of its prowess should have power to divert my companions' eyes from the bosky flanks of Devonshire combes. The little watering-place of Ilfracombe is seated at the lower verge of one of the seaward-plunging valleys, between a couple of magnificent headlands which hold it in a hollow slope and offer it securely to the caress of the Bristol Channel. It is a very finished little specimen of its genus, and I think that during my short stay there, I expended as much attention on its manners and customs and its social physiognomy as on its cliffs and beach and great coast-view. My chief conclusion, perhaps, from all these things, was that the terrible summer question which works annual anguish in so many American households would be vastly simplified if we had a few Ilfracombes scattered along our Atlantic coast; and furthermore, that the English are masters of the art of uniting the picturesque with the comfortable—in such proportions, at least, as may claim the applause of a race whose success has as yet been confined to an ingenious combination of their opposites. It is just possible that at Ilfracombe the comfortable weighs down the scale; so very substantial is it, so very officious and business-like. On the left of the town (to give an example), one of the great cliffs I have mentioned rises in a couple of massive peaks, and presents to the sea an almost vertical face, all veiled in tufts of golden brown and mighty fern. You have not walked fifty yards away from the hotel before you encounter half a dozen little signboards, directing your steps to a path up the cliff. You follow their indications, and you arrive at a little gate-house, with photographs and various local gimcracks exposed for sale. A most respectable person appears, demands a penny, and, on receiving it, admits you with great civility to commune with nature. You detect, however, various little influences hostile to perfect communion. You are greeted by another signboard threatening legal pursuit if you attempt to evade the payment of the sacramental penny. The path, winding in a hundred ramifications over the cliff, is fastidiously solid and neat, and furnished at intervals of a dozen yards with excellent benches, inscribed by knife and pencil with the names of such visitors as do not happen to have been the elderly maiden ladies who now chiefly occupy them. All this is prosaic, and you have to subtract it in a lump from the total impression before the sense of pure nature becomes distinct. Your subtraction made, a great deal assuredly remains; quite enough, I found, to give me an ample day's entertainment, for English scenery, like everything else that England produces, is of a quality that wears well. The cliffs are superb, the play of light and shade upon them a perpetual study, and the air a delicious mixture of the mountain-breeze and the sea-breeze. I was very glad at the end of my climb to have a good bench to sit upon—as one must think twice in England before measuring one's length on the grassy earth; and to be able, thanks to the smooth footpath, to get back to the hotel in a quarter of an hour. But it occurred to me that if I were an Englishman of the period, and, after ten months of a busy London life, my fancy were turning to a holiday, to rest, and change, and oblivion of the ponderous social burden, it might find rather less inspiration than needful in a vision of the little paths of Ilfracombe, of the signboards and the penny-fee and the solitude tempered by old ladies and sheep. I wondered whether change perfect enough to be salutary does not imply something more pathless, more idle, more unreclaimed from that deep-bosomed Nature to which the overwrought mind reverts with passionate longing; something in short which is attainable at a moderate distance from New York and Boston. I must add that I cannot find in my heart to object, even on grounds the most aesthetic, to the very beautiful and excellent hotel at Ilfracombe, where such of my readers as are perchance actually wrestling with the summer question may be interested to learn that one may live *en pension*, very well indeed, at a cost of ten shillings a day. I have paid very much more at some of our more modest summer resorts for very much less. I made the acquaintance at this establishment of that somewhat anomalous institution, the British *table d'hôte*, but I confess that, faithful to the duty of a sentimental tourist, I have retained a more vivid impression of the talk and the faces than of our *entrées* and *relevés*. I noticed here what I have often noticed before (the fact perhaps has never been duly recognized), that no people profit so eagerly as the English by the suspension of a common social law. A *table d'hôte*, being something abnormal and experimental, as it were, it produced, apparently, a complete reversal of the national characteristics. Conversation was universal—uproarious, almost; and I have met no vivacious Latin more confidential than a certain neighbor of mine; no speculative Yankee more inquisitive.

These are meagre memories, however, compared with those which cluster about that enchanting spot which is known in vulgar prose as Lynton. I am afraid I should seem an even more sentimental tourist than I pretend to be if I were to declare how vulgar all prose appears to me applied to Lynton with descriptive intent. The little village is perched on the side of one of the great mountain cliffs with which this whole coast is adorned, and on the edge of a lovely gorge through which a broad hill-torrent foams and tumbles from the great moors whose heather-crested waves rise purple along the inland sky. Below it, close beside the beach, where the little torrent meets the sea, is the sister village of Lynmouth. Here—as I stood on the bridge that spans the stream and looked at the strong backs and foundations and overclambering garden verdure of certain little gray old houses which plunge their feet into it, and then up at the tender green of scrub-oak and ferns and the flaming yellow of golden broom climbing the sides of the hills, and leaving them bare-crowned to the sun, like miniature mountains—I could have fancied the British Channel as blue as the Mediterranean and the village about me one of the hundred hamlets of the Riviera. The little *Castle* hotel at Lynton is a spot so consecrated to delicious repose—to sitting with a book in the terrace garden among blooming plants of aristocratic magnitude and rarity, and watching the finest piece of color in all nature—the glowing red and green of the great cliffs beyond the little harbor-mouth, as they shift and change and melt the livelong day, from shade to shade and ineffable tone to tone—that I feel as if in helping it to publicity I were doing it rather a disfavor than a service. It is in fact a very charming little abiding-place, and I have never known one where purchased hospitality wore a more disinterested smile. Lynton is of course a capital centre for excursions, but two or three of which I had time to make. None is more beautiful than a simple walk along the running face of the cliffs to a singular rocky eminence where curious abutments and pinnacles of stone have caused it to be named the "Castle." It has a fantastic resemblance to some hoary feudal ruin, with crumbling towers and gaping chambers, tenanted by wild sea-birds. The late afternoon light had a way, while I was at Lynton, of lingering on until within a couple of hours of midnight, and I remember among the charmed moments of English travel none of a more vividly poetical tinge than a couple of evenings spent on the summit of this all but legendary pile, in company with the slow-coming darkness, and the short, sharp cry of the sea-mews. There are places whose very aspect is a story. This jagged and pinnacled crust-wall, with the rock-strewn valley behind it, into the shadow of one of whose boulders, in the foreground, the glance wandered in search of the lurking signature of Gustave Doré, belonged certainly, if not to history, to legend. As I sat watching the sullen calmness of the unbroken tide at the dreadful base of the cliffs (where they divide into low sea-caves, making pillars and pedestals for the fantastic imagery of their summits), I kept for ever repeating, as if they contained a spell, half a dozen words from Tennyson's "Idylls of the King":

"On wild Tintagil, by the Cornish Sea."

False as they were to the scene geographically, they seemed somehow to express its essence; and, at any rate, I leave it to any one who has lingered there with the lingering twilight to say whether you can respond to the almost mystical picturesqueness of the place better than by spouting some sonorous line from an English poet.

The last stage in my visit to North Devon was the long drive along the beautiful remnant of coast and through the rich pastoral scenery of Somerset. The whole broad spectacle that one dreams of viewing in a foreign land, to the homely music of a post-boy's whip, I saw on this admirable drive—breezy highlands clad in the warm blue-brown of heather-tufts, as if in mantles of rusty velvet, little bays and coves curving gently to the doors of clustered fishing-huts, deep pastures and broad forests, villages thatched and trellised as if to take a prize for local color, manor-tops peeping over rook-haunted avenues. I ought to make especial note of an hour I spent at mid-day at the little village of Porlock, in Somerset. Here the thatch seemed steeper and heavier, the yellow roses on the cottage walls more cunningly mated with the crumbling stucco, the dark interiors within the open doors more quaintly pictorial, than elsewhere; and as I loitered, while the horses rested, in the little cool old timber-steepled, yew-shaded church, betwixt the grim-seated manorial pew and the battered tomb of a crusading knight and his lady, and listened to the simple prattle of a blue-eyed old sexton, who showed me where, as a boy, in scantier corduroys, he had scratched his name on the recumbent lady's breast, it seemed to me that this at last was old England indeed, and that in a moment more I should see Sir Roger de Coverley marching up the aisle; for certainly, to give a proper account of it all, I should need nothing less than the pen of Mr. Addison.

A EUROPEAN SUMMER:
WELLS AND SALISBURY

August 1872

Abbey, Glastonbury, England.

THE PLEASANTEST THINGS IN LIFE, AND PERHAPS THE RAREST, are its agreeable surprises. Things are often worse than we expect to find them, and when they are better, we may mark the day with a white stone. These reflections are as pertinent to the fortunes of man as a tourist as to any other phase of his destiny, and I recently had occasion to make them in the ancient city of Wells. I knew in a general way that it had a grand cathedral to show, but I was far from suspecting the precious picturesqueness of the little town. The immense predominance of the minster towers; as you see them from the approaching train, over the clustered houses at their feet, gives you indeed an intimation of it, and suggests that the city is nothing if not ecclesiastical; but I can wish the traveller no better fortune than to stroll forth in the early evening with as large a reserve of ignorance as my own, and treat himself to an hour of discoveries. I was lodged on the edge of Cathedral Green, and I had only to pass beneath one of the three crumbling Priory Gates which enclose it, and cross the vast grassy oval, to stand before a minster-front which ranks among the first three or four in England. Wells Cathedral is extremely fortunate in being approached by this wide green level, on which the spectator may loiter and stroll to and fro, and shift his standpoint to his heart's content. The spectator who doesn't hesitate to avail himself of his privilege of unlimited fastidiousness might indeed pronounce it too isolated for perfect picturesqueness— too uncontrasted with the profane architecture of the human homes for which it pleads to the skies. But, in fact, Wells is not a city with a Cathedral for a central feature; but a Cathedral with a little city gathered at its base, and forming hardly more than an extension of its spacious Close. You feel everywhere the presence of the beautiful church; the place seems always to savor of a Sunday afternoon; and you fancy that every house is tenanted by a canon, a prebendary, or a precentor.

The great *façade* is remarkable not so much for its expanse as for its elaborate elegance. It consists of two great truncated towers, divided by a broad centre bearing beside its rich fretwork of statues three narrow lancet windows. The statues on this vast front are the great boast of the Cathedral. They number, with the lateral figures of the towers, no less than three hundred; it seems densely embroidered by the chisel. They are disposed in successive niches, along six main vertical shafts; the central windows are framed and divided by narrower shafts, and the wall above them rises into a pinnacled screen, traversed by two superb horizontal rows. Add to these a close-running cornice of images along the line corresponding with the summit of the aisles, and the tiers which complete the decoration of the towers on either side, and you have an immense system of images, governed by a quaint theological order and most impressing in its completeness. Many of the little high-lodged effigies are mutilated, and not a few of the niches are empty, but the injury of time is not sufficient to diminish the noble serenity of the building. The injury of time is indeed being handsomely repaired, for the front is partly masked by a slender scaffolding. The props and platforms are of the most delicate structure, and look in fact as if they were meant to facilitate no more ponderous labor than a fitting-on of noses to disfeatured bishops, and a rearrangement of the mantle-folds of strait-laced queens, discomposed by the centuries. The main beauty of Wells Cathedral, to my mind, is not its more or less visible wealth of detail, but its singularly charm-ing tone of color. An even, sober, mouse-colored gray covers it from summit to base, deepening nowhere to the melancholy black of your truly romantic Gothic, but showing, as yet, none of the spotty brightness of "restoration." It is a wonderful fact that the great towers, from their lofty outlook, see never a factory chimney—those cloud-compelling spires which so often break the charm of the softest English horizons; and the general atmo-sphere of Wells seemed to me, for some reason, peculiarly lumi-nous and sweet. The Cathedral has never been discolored by the moral malaria of a city with an independent secular life. As you turn back from its portal and glance at the open lawn before it, edged by the mild gray Elizabethan Deanery and the dwellings hardly less stately which seem to reflect in their comfortable fronts the rich respectability of the church, and then up again at the beautiful clear-hued pile, you may fancy it less a temple for man's needs than a monument of his pride—less a fold for the flock than for the shepherds—a visible sign that beside the actual assortment of heavenly thrones, there is constantly on hand a choice lot of cushioned cathedral stalls. Within the Ca-thedral this impression is not diminished. The interior is vast and massive, but it lacks incident—the incident of monuments, sepulchres, and chapels—and it is too brilliantly lighted for pic-turesque, as distinguished from strictly architectural, interest. Under this latter head it has, I believe, great importance. For myself, I can think of it only as I saw it from my place in the choir during afternoon service of a hot Sunday. The Bishop sat facing me, enthroned in a stately Gothic alcove, and clad in his crimson band, his *manches bouffantes*, and his lavender gloves; the canons, in their degree, with the archdeacons, as I suppose, reclined comfortably in the carven stalls, and the scanty congregation fringed the broad aisle. But though scanty, the congregation was select; it was unexceptionably black-coated, bonneted, and gloved. It savored intensely, in short, of that inexorable gentility which the English put on with their Sunday bonnets and beavers, and which fills me—as a purely sentimental tourist—with a sort of fond reactionary remembrance of those animated bundles of rags which one sees kneeling in the churches of Italy. But even here, as a purely sentimental tourist, I found my account: one always does in some little corner in England. Before me and beside me sat a row of the comeliest young men, clad in black gowns, and wearing on their shoulders long hoods trimmed with white fur. Who and what they were I know not, for I preferred not to learn, lest by chance they should not be as mediaeval as they looked.

My fancy found its account even better in the singular quaintness of the little precinct known as the Vicars' Close. It directly adjoins the Cathedral Green, and you enter it beneath one of the solid old gate-houses which form so striking an element in the ecclesiastical furniture of Wells. It consists of a narrow, oblong court, bordered on each side with thirteen small dwellings, and terminating in a ruinous little chapel. Here formerly dwelt a congregation of Vicars, established in the thirteenth century to do curates' work for the canons. The little houses are very much modernized; but they retain their tall chimneys, with carven tablets in the face, their antique compactness and neatness, and a certain little sanctified air, as of cells in a cloister. The place is deliciously picturesque, and approaching it as I did, in the first dimness of twilight, it looked to me, in its exaggerated perspective, like one of those "streets" represented on the stage, down whose impossible vista the heroes and confidants of romantic comedies come swaggering arm-in-arm, and hold amorous converse with the heroines at second-story windows. But though the Vicars' Close is a curious affair enough, the great boast of Wells is its Episcopal Palace. The Palace loses nothing from being seen for the first time in the kindly twilight, and from being approached with an unexpectant mind. To reach it (unless you go from within the Cathedral by the cloisters), you pass out of the Green by another ancient gateway into the market-place, and thence back again through its own peculiar portal. My own first glimpse of it had all the felicity of a *coup de théâtre*. I saw within the dark archway an enclosure bedimmed at once with the shadows of trees and heightened with the glitter of water. The picture was worthy of this agreeable promise. Its main feature is the little gray-walled island on which the Palace stands, rising in feudal fashion out of a broad, clear moat, flanked with round towers, and approached by a proper drawbridge. Along the outer side of the moat is a short walk beneath a row of picturesquely stunted elms; swans and ducks disport themselves in the current and ripple the bright shadows of the overclambering plants from the episcopal gardens and masses of purple valerian lodged on the hoary battlements. On the evening of my visit, the haymakers were at work on a great sloping field in the rear of the Palace, and the sweet perfume of the tumbled grass in the dusky air seemed all that was wanting to fix the scene for ever in the memory. Beyond the moat, and within the gray walls, dwells my Lord Bishop, in the finest palace in England. The mansion dates from the thirteenth century; but, stately dwelling though it is, it occupies but a subordinate place in its own grounds. Their great ornament, picturesquely speaking, is the massive ruin of a banqueting-hall, erected by a free-living mediaeval bishop, and more or less demolished at the Reformation. With its still perfect towers and beautiful shapely windows, hung with those green tapestries so stoutly woven by the English climate, it is a relic worthy of being locked away behind an embattled wall. I have among my impressions of Wells, besides this picture of the moated Palace, half a dozen memories of the pictorial sort, which I lack space to transcribe. The clearest impression, perhaps, is that of the beautiful church of St. Cuthbert, of the same date as the Cathedral, and in very much the same style of elegant, temperate Early English. It wears one of the high-soaring towers for which Somersetshire is justly celebrated, as you may see from the window of the train as you roll past its almost top-heavy hamlets. The beautiful old church, surrounded with its green graveyard, and large enough to be impressive, without being too large (a great merit, to my sense) to be easily compassed by a deplorably unarchitectural eye, were a native English expression, to which certain humble figures in the foreground gave additional point. On the edge of the churchyard was a low-gabled house, before which four old men were gossiping in the eventide. Into the front of the house was inserted an antique alcove in stone, divided into three shallow little seats, two of which were occupied by extraordinary specimens of decrepitude. One of these ancient paupers had a huge protuberant forehead and sat with a pensive air, his head gathered painfully upon his twisted shoulders, and his legs resting across his crutch. The other was rubicund, blear-eyed, and frightfully besmeared with snuff. Their voices were so feeble and senile that I could scarcely understand them, and only just managed to make out the answer to my enquiry of who and what they were—"We're Still's Almshouse, sir."

One of the lions, almost, of Wells (whence it is but five miles distant) is the ruin of the famous Abbey of Glastonbury, on which Henry VIII, in the language of our day, came down so heavily. The ancient splendor of the architecture survives, but in scattered and scanty fragments, among influences of a rather inharmonious sort. It was cattle-market in the little town as I passed up the main street, and a savor of hoofs and hide seemed to accompany me through the simple labyrinth of the old arches and piers. These occupy a large back-yard close behind the street, to which you are most prosaically admitted by a young woman who keeps a wicket and sells tickets. The continuity of tradition is not altogether broken, however, for the little street of Glastonbury has rather an old-time aspect, and one of the houses at least must have seen the last of the Abbots ride abroad on his mule. The little inn is a capital bit of picturesqueness, and as I waited for the 'bus under its low dark archway (in something of the mood, possibly, in which a train was once waited for at Coventry), and watched the barmaid flirting her way to and fro out of the heavy-browed kitchen and among the lounging young appraisers of colts and steers and barmaids, I might have imagined that the merry England of the Tudors was not utterly dead. A beautiful England this must have been as well, if it contained many such abbeys as Glastonbury. Such of the ruined columns and portals and windows as still remain are of admirable design and finish. The doorways are rich in marginal ornament—ornament within ornament, as it often is; for the dainty weeds and wild flowers overlace the antique tracery with their bright arabesques and deepen the gray of the stonework, as it brightens their bloom. The thousand flowers which grow among English ruins deserve a chapter to themselves. I owe them, as an observer, a heavy debt of satisfaction, but I am too little of a botanist to pay them in their own coin. It has often seemed to me in England that the purest enjoyment of architecture was to be had among the ruins of great buildings. In the perfect building one is rarely sure that the impression is simply architectural: it is more or less pictorial and sentimental; it depends partly upon association and partly upon various accessories and details which, however they may be wrought into harmony with the architectural idea, are not part of its essence of spirit. But in so far as beauty of structure is beauty of line and curve, balance and harmony of masses and dimensions, I have seldom relished it as deeply as on the grassy nave of some crumbling church, before lonely columns and empty windows, where the wild flowers were a cornice and the cloudy sky a roof. The arts certainly have a common element. These hoary relics of Glastonbury reminded me in their broken eloquence of one of the other great ruins of the world—the "Last Supper" of Leonardo. A beautiful shadow, in each case, is all that remains; but that shadow is the artist's thought.

Salisbury Cathedral, to which I made a pilgrimage on leaving Wells, is the very reverse of a ruin, and you take your pleasure there on very different grounds from those I have just attempted to define. It is perhaps the best known cathedral in the world, thanks to its shapely spire; but the spire is so simply and obviously fair that when you have frankly made your bow to it you have anticipated aesthetic analysis. I had seen it before and admired it heartily, and perhaps I should have done as well to let my admiration rest. I confess that on repeated inspection it grew to seem to me the least bit *banal*, as the French say, and I began to consider whether it doesn't belong to the same range of art as the Apollo Belvidere or the Venus de' Medici. I incline to think that if I had to live within sight of a cathedral and encounter it in my daily comings and goings, I should grow less weary of the rugged black front of Exeter than of the sweet perfection of Salisbury. There are people who become easily satiated with blonde beauties, and Salisbury Cathedral belongs, if I may say so, to the order of blondes. The other lions of Salisbury, Stonehenge and Wilton House, I revisited with undiminished interest. Stonehenge is rather a hackneyed shrine of pilgrimage. At the time of my former visit a picnic party was making libations of beer on the dreadful altar-sites. But the mighty mystery of the place has not yet been stared out of countenance, and as on this occasion there were no picnickers, we were left to drink deep of the harmony of its solemn isolation and its unrecorded past. It stands as lonely in history as it does on the great plain, whose many-tinted green waves, as they roll away from it, seem to symbolize the ebb of the long centuries which have left it so portentously unexplained. You may put a hundred questions to these rough-hewn giants as they bend in grim contemplation of their fallen companions; but your curiosity falls dead in the vast sunny stillness that enshrouds them, and the strange monument, with all its unspoken memories, becomes simply a heart-stirring picture in a land of pictures. It is indeed immensely picturesque. At a distance, you see it standing in a shallow dell of the plain, looking hardly larger than a group of ten-pins on a bowling-green. I can fancy sitting all a summer's day watching its shadows shorten and lengthen again, and drawing a delicious contrast between the world's duration and the feeble span of individual experience. There is something in Stonehenge almost reassuring, and if you are disposed to feel that life is a rather superficial matter, and that we soon get to the bottom of things, the immemorial gray pillars may serve to remind you of the enormous background of Time. Salisbury is indeed rich in antiquities. Wilton House, a most comely old residence of the Earl of Pembroke, preserves a noble collection of Greek and Roman marbles. These are ranged round a charming cloister, occupying the centre of the house, which is exhibited in the most liberal fashion. Out of the cloister opens a series of drawing-rooms hung with family portraits, chiefly by Van Dyck, all of superlative merit. Among them hangs supreme, as the Van Dyck *par excellence*, the famous and magnificent group of the whole Pembroke family of James I's time. This splendid work has every pictorial merit—design, color, elegance, force, and finish, and I have been vainly wondering to this hour what it needs to be the finest piece of portraiture, as it surely is one of the most ambitious, in the world. What it lacks, characteristically, in a certain uncompromising solidity it recovers in the beautiful dignity of its position—unmoved from the stately house in which its authors sojourned and wrought, familiar to the descendants of its noble originals.

A EUROPEAN SUMMER:
FROM CHAMBERY TO MILAN
November 1872

Sketch of "Les Charmettes," ca. 1830.

Your truly sentimental tourist can never *bouder* long, and it was at Chambéry—but four hours from Geneva—that I accepted the situation, and decided that there might be mysterious delights in entering Italy whizzing through an eight-mile tunnel, like some highly-improved projectile of the period. I found my reward in the Savoyard landscape, which greets you betimes with something of a Southern smile. If it is not as Italian as Italy, it is, at least, more Italian than Switzerland—more Italian, too, I should think, than can seem natural and proper to the swarming red-legged soldiery who so ostentatiously assign it to the dominion of M. Thiers. The light and coloring had, to my eyes, not a little of that mollified depth which they had last observed in Italy. It was simply, perhaps, that the weather was hot and that the mountains were drowsing in that iridescent haze which I have seen nearer home than at Chambéry. But the vegetation, assuredly, had an all but Trans-alpine twist and curl, and the classic wayside tangle of corn and vines left nothing to be desired in the line of careless grace. Chambéry as a town, however, affords little premonition of It-aly. There is shabbiness and shabbiness, the discriminating tourist will tell you; and that of the ancient capital of Savoy lacks color. I found a better pastime, however, than strolling through the dark, dull streets in quest of "effects" that were not forthcoming. The first urchin you meet will tell you the way to Les Charmettes and the Maison Jean-Jacques. A very pleasant way it becomes as soon as it leaves the town—a winding, climb-ing by-road, bordered with such a tall and sturdy hedge as to give it the air of an English lane—if you can fancy an English lane introducing you to the haunts of a Madame de Warens! The house which formerly sheltered this lady's singular *ménage* stands on a hillside above the road, which a rapid path connects with the little grass-grown terrace before it. It is a small, shabby, homely dwelling, with a certain reputable solidity, however, and more of internal spaciousness than of outside promise. The place is shown by an elderly Frenchwoman, who points out the very few surviving objects which you may touch, with the reflection—complacent in whatsoever degree suits you—that Rousseau's hand has often lain there. It was presumably a meagrely-appointed house, and I wondered that on these scanty features so much expression should linger. But the edifice has an ancient ponderosity of structure, and the dust of the eighteenth century seems to lie on its worm-eaten floors, to cling to the faded old *papiers à ramages* on the walls, and to lodge in the crevices of the brown wooden ceilings. Madame de Warens's bed remains, with Rousseau's own narrow couch, his little warped and cracked yellow spinet, and a battered, turnip-shaped silver timepiece, engraved with its master's name—its primitive tick as extinct as his heart-beats. It cost me, I confess, a somewhat pitying acceleration of my own to see this intimately personal relic of the *genius loci*—for it had dwelt in his waistcoat pocket, than which there is hardly a material point in space nearer to a man's consciousness—tossed so irreverently upon the table on which you deposited your fee, beside the dog's-eared visitors' record—the *livre de cuisine* recently denounced by Madame Sand. In fact, the place generally, in so far as some faint ghostly presence of its famous inmates seems to linger there, is by no means exhilarating. Coppet and Ferney tell, if not of pure happiness, at least of prosperity and honor, wealth and success. But Les Charmettes is haunted by ghosts unclean and forlorn. The place tells of poverty, trouble, and impurity. A good deal of clever modern talent in France has been employed in touching up the episode of which it was the scene, and tricking it out in idyllic love-knots. But as I stand on the charming terrace I have mentioned—a little jewel of a terrace, with grassy flags and a mossy parapet, and an admirable view of great swelling violet hills—stand there reminded how much sweeter Nature is than man, the story looked rather wan and unlovely beneath these literary decorations, and I could muster no keener relish for it than is implied in perfect pity. Hero and heroine were first-rate subjects for psychology, but hardly for poetry. But, not to moralize too sternly for a tourist between trains, I should add that, as an illustration to be inserted mentally in the text of the "Confessions," a glimpse of Les Charmettes is pleasant enough. It completes the rare charm of good autobiography to behold with one's eyes the faded and battered *mise en scène* of the story; and Rousseau's narrative is so incomparably vivid and forcible, that the sordid little house at Chambéry seems of a hardly deeper shade of reality than the images you contemplate in his pages.

If I spent an hour at Les Charmettes, fumbling thus helplessly with the past, I frankly recognized on the morrow that the Mont Cenis Tunnel savors strongly of the future. As I passed along the St. Gothard, a couple of months since, I perceived, halfway up the Swiss ascent, a group of navvies at work in a gorge beneath the road. They had laid bare a broad surface of granite, and had punched in the centre of it a round, black cavity of about the dimensions, as it seemed to me, of a soup-plate. This was the embryonic form of the dark mid-channel of the St. Gothard Railway, which is to attain its perfect development some eight years hence. The Mont Genis, therefore, may be held to have set a fashion which will be followed till the highest Himalaya is but the ornamental apex or snow-capped gable-tip of some re-sounding fuliginous corridor. The tunnel differs but in length from other tunnels; you spend half an hour in it. But you come whizzing out of it into Transalpine Italy, and, as you look back, may fancy it shrugging its mighty shoulders over the track—a spasmodic protest of immobility against speed. The tunnel is certainly not a poetic object, but there is no perfection without its beauty; and as you measure the long rugged outline of the pyramid of which it forms the base, you must admit that it is the perfection of a short cut. Twenty-four hours from Paris to Turin is speed for the times—speed which may content us, at any rate, until expansive Berlin has succeeded in placing itself at thirty-six from Milan. I entered Turin of a lovely August afternoon, and found a city of arcades, of pink and yellow stucco, of innu-merable cafés, blue-legged officers, and ladies draped in the Spanish veil. An old friend of Italy, coming back to her, finds an easy waking for sleeping memories. Every object is a reminder.

Half an hour after my arrival, as I stood at my window, looking out on the great square, it seemed to me that the scene within and without was a rough *résumé* of every pleasure and every impression I had formerly gathered from Italy: the balcony and the venetian-blind, the cool floor of speckled concrete, the lavish delusions of frescoed wall and ceiling, the broad divan framed for the noonday siesta, the massive mediaeval Castello in mid-square, with its shabby rear and its pompous Palladian front, the brick *campaniles* beyond, the milder, yellower light, the brighter colors and softer sounds. Later, beneath the arcades, I found many an old acquaintance, beautiful officers, resplendent, slow-strolling, contemplative of female beauty; civil and peaceful dandies, hardly less gorgeous, with that religious faith in their moustaches and shirt-fronts which distinguishes the *belle jeunesse* of Italy; ladies most artfully veiled in lace mantillas, but with too little art—or too much nature, at least—in the region of the *corsage*; well-conditioned young *abati*, with neatly-drawn stockings. These, indeed, are not objects of first-rate interest, and with such Turin is rather meagerly furnished. It has no architecture, no churches, no monuments, nor especially picturesque street-scenery. It has, indeed, the great votive temple of the Superga, which stands on a high hilltop above the city, gazing across at Monte Rosa, and lifting its own fine dome against the sky with no contemptible art. But when you have seen the Superga from the quay beside the Po, as shrivelled and yellow in

August as some classic Spanish stream, and said to yourself that in architecture position is half the battle, you have nothing left to visit but the Museum of pictures. The Turin Gallery, which is large and well arranged, is the fortunate owner of three or four masterpieces; a couple of magnificent Van Dycks and a couple of Paul Veroneses; the latter a Queen of Sheba and a Feast at the House of Levi—the usual splendid combination of brocades, grandees, and marble colonnades dividing skies *de turquoise malade*, as Théophile Gautier says. The Veroneses are fine, but with Venice in prospect the traveller feels at liberty to keep his best attention in reserve. If, however, he has the proper relish for Van Dyck, let him linger long and fondly here; for that admiration will never be more potently stirred than by the delicious picture of the three little royal highnesses, daughters of Charles I. All the purity of childhood is here, and all its soft solidity of structure, rounded tenderly beneath the spangled satin, and contrasted charmingly with its pompous rigidity. The little princesses, clad respectively in crimson, white, and blue, stand up in their ruffs and fardingales in dimpled serenity, squaring their infantine stomachers at the spectator with an innocence, a dignity, a delightful grotesqueness, which make the picture as real as it is elegant. You might kiss their hands, but you certainly would think twice before pinching their cheeks—provocative as they are of this tribute of admiration—and would altogether lack presumption to lift them off the ground—the royal dais on which they stand so sturdily planted *par droit de naissance*. There is something inimitable in the paternal gallantry with which the painter has touched off these imposing little ladies. They were babies, yet they were princesses, and he has contrived, we may fancy, to work into his picture an intimation that they were creatures whom, in their teens, the lucklessly smitten—even as he was prematurely—must vainly sigh for. Although the work is a masterpiece of execution, its merits under this head may be emulated—at a distance. The lovely modulations of color in the three contrasted and harmonized little satin petticoats—the solidity of the little heads, in spite of all their prettiness—the happy, unexaggerated squareness and maturity of *pose*—are, severally, points to study, to imitate, and to reproduce with profit. But the *taste* of the picture is its great secret as well as its great merit—a taste which seems one of the lost instincts of mankind. Go and enjoy this supreme expression of Van Dyck's fine sense, and admit that never was a politer work.

Milan is an older, richer, more historic city than Turin; but its general aspect is no more distinctly Italian. The long Austrian occupation, perhaps, did something to Germanize its physiognomy; though, indeed, this is an indifferent explanation when one remembers how well, picturesquely, Italy held its own in Venetia. Far be it from me, moreover, to accuse Milan of a want of picturesqueness. I mean simply that at certain points it seems rather like the last of the Northern capitals than the

first of the Southern. The cathedral is before all things picturesque; it is not interesting, it is not logical, it is not even, to
some minds, commandingly beautiful; but it is grandly curious,
superbly rich. I hope, for my own part, that I shall never grow
too fastidious to enjoy it. If it had no other beauty it would have
that of impressive, immeasurable achievement. As I strolled beside its vast indented base one evening, and felt it above me,
massing its grey mysteries in the starlight, while the restless human tide on which I floated rose no higher than the first great
block of street-soiled marble, I was tempted to believe that
beauty in great architecture is almost a secondary merit, and
that the main point is mass—such mass as may make it a supreme embodiment of sustained effort. Viewed in this way, a
great building is the greatest conceivable work of art. More than
any other it represents difficulties annulled, resources combined,
labor, courage, and patience. And there are people who tell us
that art has nothing to do with morality. Little enough, doubtless, when it is concerned, over so little, in painting the roof of
Milan Cathedral within to represent carved stone-work. Of this
famous roof every one has heard—how good it is, how bad, how
perfect a delusion, how transparent an artifice. It is the first
thing your *valet de place* shows you on entering the church. The
discriminating tourist may accept it philosophically, I think; for
the interior, though admirably effective, has no very recondite
beauties. It is splendidly vast and dim; the altar-lamps twinkle

afar through the incense-thickened air like fog-lights at sea, and the great columns rise straight to the roof, which hardly curves to meet them, with the girth and altitude of oaks of a thousand years; but there is little refinement of design—few of those felicities of proportion which the eye caresses, when it finds them, very much as the memory retains and repeats some happy line of poetry or some delightful musical phrase. But picturesque, I repeat, is the whole vast scene, and nothing more so than a certain exhibition which I privately enjoyed of the relics of St. Charles Borromeo. This holy man lies at his eternal rest in a small but gorgeous sepulchral chapel, beneath the pavement of the church, before the high altar; and, for the modest sum of five francs, you may have his shrivelled mortality unveiled, and gaze at it in all the dreadful double scepticism of a Protestant and a tourist. The Catholic Church, I believe, has some doctrine that its ends justify at need any means whatsoever; *a fortiori*, therefore, nothing it does can be ridiculous. The performance in question, of which the good San Carlo *fit les frais*, as the French say, was impressive, certainly, but as great grotesqueness is impressive. The little sacristan, having secured his audience, whipped on a white tunic over his frock, lighted a couple of extra candles, and proceeded to remove from above the altar, by means of a crank, a sort of sliding shutter, just as you may see a shop-boy do of a morning at his master's window. In this case, too, a large sheet of plate-glass was uncovered, and, to form an idea of the étalage, you must imagine that a jeweller, for reasons of his own, has struck an unnatural partnership with an undertaker. The black, mummified corpse of the saint is stretched out in a glass coffin, clad in his mouldering canonicals, mitred, crosiered, and gloved, and glittering with votive jewels. It is an extraordinary mixture of death and life; the desiccated clay, the ashen rags, the hideous little black mask and skull, and the living, glowing, twinkling splendor of diamonds, emeralds, and sapphires. The collection is really fine, and various great historic names are attached to the different offerings. Whatever may be the better opinion as to whether the Church is in a decline, I cannot help thinking that she will make a tolerable figure in the world so long as she retains this great capital of bric-a-brac, scintillating throughout Christendom at effectively scattered points. You see, I am forced to agree after all, in spite of the sliding shutter and the profane exhibitory arts of the sacristan, that the majesty of the Church saved the situation, or made it, at least, sublimely ridiculous. Yet it was from a natural desire to breathe a sweeter air that I immediately afterwards undertook the interminable climb to the roof of the cathedral. This is a great spectacle, and one of the best known; for every square inch of wall on the winding stairways is bescribbled with a traveller's name. There is a great glare from the far-stretching slopes of marble, a confusion (like the masts of a navy or the spears of an army) of image-capped pinnacles, biting the impalpable blue, and, better than either, a delicious view of level Lombardy, sleeping in its rich Transalpine light, and looking, with its white-walled dwellings, and the spires on its horizon, like a vast green sea spotted with ships. After two months of Switzerland, the Lombard plain is a delicious rest to the eye, and the yellow, liquid, free-flowing light (as if in favored Italy the vessels of heaven were more widely opened) had for mine a charm which made me think of a great opaque mountain as a blasphemous invasion of the atmospheric spaces.

I have mentioned the cathedral first, but the prime treasure of Milan at the present hour is the beautiful, tragical Leonardo. The cathedral is good for another thousand years, but I doubt that our children will find in the most majestic and most luckless of frescoes much more than the shadow of a shadow. Its frame for many years now has been that, as one may say, of an illustrious invalid whom people visit to see how he lasts, with deathbed speeches: The picture needs not another scar or stain, now, to be the saddest work of art in the world, and battered, defaced, ruined as it is, it remains one of the greatest. It is really not amiss to compare its decay to the slow extinction of a human organism. The creation of the picture was a breath from the infinite, and the painter's conception not immeasurably less complex than that involved, say, in his own personality. There has been much talk lately about the irony of fate, but I doubt that fate was ever more ironical than when she led this most deeply calculating of artists to spend fifteen long years in building his goodly house upon the sand. And yet, after all, can I fancy this apparent irony but a deeper wisdom, for if the picture enjoyed the immortal health and bloom of a first-rate Titian we should have lost one of the most pertinent lessons in the history of art. We know it as hearsay, but here is the plain proof, that there is no limit to the amount of substance an artist may put into his work. Every painter ought once in his life to stand before the *Cenacolo* and decipher its moral. Pour everything you mentally possess into your picture, lest perchance your "prepared surface" should play you a trick! Raphael was a happier genius; you cannot look at his lovely Marriage of the Virgin at the Brera, beautiful as some first deep smile of conscious inspiration, without feeling that he foresaw no complaint against fate, and that he looked at the world with the vision of a graceful optimist. But I have left no space to speak of the Brera, nor of that paradise of bookworms with an eye for the picturesque—if such creatures exist—the Ambrosian Library; nor of that solid old basilica of St. Ambrose, with its spacious atrium and its crudely solemn mosaics, in which it is surely your own fault if you don't forget Dr. Strauss and M. Renan, and worship as simply as a Christian of the ninth century.

It is part of the sordid prose of the Mont Cenis road that, unlike those fine old unimproved passes, the Simplon, the Splügen, and—yet awhile longer—the St. Gothard, it denies you a glimpse of that paradise adorned by the three lakes as that of uncommented Scripture by the rivers of Eden. I made, however, from Milan an excursion to the Lake of Como which, though brief, lasted long enough to make me feel as if I, too, were a hero of romance, with leisure for a *grande passion*, and not a hurrying tourist with a "Bradshaw" in his pocket. The Lake of Como has figured largely in fiction of the sentimental sort. It is commonly the spot to which ardent young gentlemen are wont to invite the wives of other gentlemen to fly with them, and ignore the cold obstruction of public opinion. But here is a chance for the stern moralist to rejoice; the Lake of Como, too, has been improved, and can boast of a public opinion. I should pay a poor compliment, at least, to the swarming inmates of the hotels which now alternate gracefully by the waterside, with villas old and new, to think that it could not. But if it is lost to old-fashioned romance, the unsophisticated American tourist may still find delicious entertainment there. The pretty hotel at Cadenabbia offers him at least the romance of what we call at home summer board. It is all so unreal, so fictitious, so elegant and idle, so framed to undermine a rigid sense of the chief end of man not being to float for ever in an ornamental boat, beneath an awning tasselled like a circus-horse, impelled by an affable Giovanni or Antonio from one stately stretch of lake-laved villa steps to another, that departure seems as harsh and unnatural as the dream-dispelling note of some punctual voice at your bedside on a dusky winter morning. Yet I wondered, for my own part, where I had seen it all before—the pink-walled villas gleaming through their shrubberies of orange and oleander, the mountains shimmering in the hazy light like so many breasts of doves, the constant presence of the melodious Italian voice. Where, indeed, but at the Opera, when the manager has been more than usually regardless of expense? Here, in the foreground, was the palace of the nefarious barytone, with its banqueting hall opening as freely on the stage as a railway buffet on the platform; beyond, the delightful back scene, with its operatic gamut of coloring; in the middle, the scarlet-sashed *barcaiuoli*, grouped like a chorus, hat in hand, awaiting the conductor's signal. It was better even than being in a novel—this being in a *libretto*.

THE PARISIAN STAGE
December 7, 1872

Interior of the Comédie-Française, as originally designed in 1790.

I T IS IMPOSSIBLE TO SPEND MANY WEEKS IN PARIS WITHOUT observing that the theatre plays a very important part in French civilization; and it is impossible to go much to the theatre without finding it a copious source of instruction as to French ideas, manners, and characters. I supposed that I had a certain acquaintance with these complex phenomena, but during the last couple of mouths I have occupied a great many *fauteuils d'orchestre*, and in the merciless glare of the footlights I have read a great many of my old convictions with a new distinctness. I have had at the same time one of the greatest attainable pleasures; for, surely, among the pleasures that one deliberately seeks and pays for, none beguiles the heavy human consciousness so totally as a first-rate evening at the Théâtre Français or the Gymnase. It was the poet Gray, I believe, who said that his idea of heaven was to lie all day on a sofa and read novels. He, poor man, spoke while "Clarissa Harlowe" was still the fashion and a novel was synonymous with an eternity. A much better heaven, I think, would be to sit all night in a *fauteuil* (if they were only a little better stuffed) listening to Delaunay, watching Got, or falling in love with Mlle. Desclée. An acted play is a novel intensified; it realizes what the novel suggests, and, by paying a liberal tribute to the senses, anticipates your possible complaint that your entertainment is of the meagre sort styled "intellectual." The stage throws into relief the best gifts of the French mind, and the Théâtre Français is not only the most amiable but the most characteristic of French institutions. I often think of the inevitable first sensations there of the "cultivated foreigner," let him be as stuffed with hostile prejudice as you please. He leaves the theatre an ardent Gallomaniac. This, he cries, is the civilized nation *par excellence*. Such art, such finish, such grace, such taste, such a marvellous exhibition of applied science, are the mark of chosen people, and these delightful talents imply the existence of every virtue. His enthusiasm may be short and make few converts; but certainly during his stay in Paris, whatever may be his mind in the intervals, he never listens to the traditional *toc-toc-toc* which sounds up the curtain in the Rue Richelieu, without murmuring, as he squares himself in his chair and grasps his *lorgnette*, that after all the French are prodigiously great!

I shall never forget a certain evening in the early summer when, after a busy, dusty, weary day in the streets, staring at charred ruins and finding in all things a vague aftertaste of gunpowder, I repaired to the Théâtre Français to listen to Molière's "Mariage Forcé," and Alfred de Musset's "Il Ne Faut Jurer de Rien." The entertainment seemed to my travel-tired brain what a perfumed bath is to one's weary limbs, and I sat in a sort of languid ecstasy of contemplation and wonder—wonder that the tender flower of poetry and art should bloom again so bravely over blood-stained garments and fresh-made graves. Molière is played at the Théâtre Français as he deserves to be—one can hardly say more—with the most ungrudging breadth, exuberance, and *entrain*, and yet with a kind of academic harmony and solemnity. Molière, if he ever drops a kindly glance on MM. Got and Coquelin, must be the happiest of the immortals. To be read two hundred years after your death is something; but to be acted is better—at least when your name doesn't happen to be Shakespeare and your interpreter the great American (or, indeed, the great British) tragedian. Such powerful, natural, wholesome comedy as that of the creator of *Sganarelle* certainly never was conceived, and the actors I have just named give it its utmost force. I have often wondered that in the keen and lucid atmosphere which Molière casts about him, some of the effusions of his modern successors should live for an hour. Alfred de Musset, however, need fear no neighborhood, and his "Il ne Faut Jurer," after Molière's tremendous farce, was like fine sherry after strong ale. Got plays in it a small part, which he makes a great one, and Delaunay, the silver-tongued, the ever-young, and that plain robust person and admirable artist, Madame Nathalie, and that divinely ingenuous *ingènue*, Mlle. Reichemberg. It would be a poor compliment to the performance to say that it might have been mistaken for real life. If real life were a tithe as charming it would be a merry world. De Musset's plays, which, in general, were not written for the stage, are of so ethereal a quality that they lose more than they gain by the interpretation, refined and sympathetic as it is, which they receive at the Théâtre Français. The most artistic acting is coarser than the poet's intention.

The play in question, however, is an exception and keeps its silvery tone even in the glare of the footlights. The second act, at the rising of the curtain, represents a drawing-room in the country; a stout, eccentric *baronne* sits with her tapestry, making distracted small talk while she counts her points with a deliciously rustic abbé; on the other side, her daughter, in white muslin and blue ribbons, is primly taking her dancing lesson from a venerable choregraphic pedagogue in a wig and tights. The exquisite art with which, for the following ten minutes, the tone of random accidental conversation is preserved, while the *baronne* loses her glasses and miscounts her stitches, and the daughter recommences her step for the thirtieth time, must simply, as the saying is, be seen to be appreciated. The acting is full of charming detail—detail of a kind we not only do not find but do not even look for on the English stage. The way in which, in a subsequent scene, the young girl, listening at evening in the park to the passionate whisperings of the hero, drops her arms half awkwardly along her sides in fascinated self-surrender, is a touch quite foreign to English invention. Unhappily for us as actors, we are not a gesticulating people. Mlle. Reichemberg's movement here is an intonation in gesture as eloquent as if she had spoken it. The incomparable Got has but a dozen short speeches to make, but he distils them with magical neatness. He sits down to piquet with the *baronne*. "You risk nothing, M. l'abbé?" she soon demands. The concentrated timorous prudence of the abbé's *"Oh! Non!"* is a master-stroke; it depicts a lifetime. Where Delaunay plays, however, it is hard not to call him the first. To say that he *satisfies* may at first seem small praise; but it may content us when we remember what a very loose fit in the poet's vision is the usual *jeune premier* of the sentimental drama. He has at best a vast deal

of fustian to utter, and he has a perilous balance to preserve between the degree of romantic expression expected in a gentleman
whose trade is love-making and the degree tolerated in a gentleman who wears a better or worse made black coat and carries the
hat of the period. Delaunay is fifty years old, and his person and
physiognomy are meagre; but his taste is so unerring, his touch so
light and true, his careless grace so free and so elegant, that in his
hands the *jeune premier* becomes a creation as fresh and natural
as the unfolding rose. He has a voice of extraordinary sweetness
and flexibility, and a delivery which makes the commonest
phrases musical, but when as *Valentin*, as *Perdican*, or as *Fortunio*,
he embarks on one of De Musset's melodious *tirades*, and his utterance melts and swells in trembling cadence and ringing em-
phasis, there is really little to choose between the performance,
as a mere vocal exhibition, and an *aria* by a first-rate tenor.

An actor equally noted for his elegance, now attested by
forty years of triumphs, is Bressant, whose name, with old Pari-
sians, is a synonym for *la distinction.* "Distingue comme Bressant"
is an accepted formula of praise. A few years ago comedians were
denied Christian burial; such are the revenges of history. Bressant's gentility is certainly a remarkable piece of art, but he always seems to me too conscious that an immense supply of the
commodity is expected from him. Nevertheless, the Théâtre
Français offers nothing more effective and suggestive than certain little comedies (the "Post Scriptum," for instance, by Emile

Augier), in which he receives the *réplique* from that venerable *grande coquette*, Mme. Plessy, the direct successor, in certain parts, of Mlle. Mars. I find these illustrious veterans, on such occasions, more interesting even than they aspire to be, and the really picturesque figures are not the Comte or the Marquise, but the grim and battered old comedians, with a life's length of footlights making strange shadows on their impenetrable masks. As a really august exhibition of experience, I recommend a *tête-à-téte* between these artists. The orchestra of the Théâtre Français is haunted by a number of old gentlemen, classic playgoers, who look as if they took snuff from boxes adorned with portraits of the fashionable beauty of 1320. I caught an echo of my impressions from one of them the other evening, when, as the curtain fell on Bressant and Plessy, he murmured ecstatically to his neighbor, "*Quelle connaissance de la scène . . . et de la vie!*"

The audience at the Parisian theatres is indeed often as interesting to me as the play. It is, of course, composed of heterogeneous elements. There are a great many ladies with red wigs in the boxes, and a great many bald young gentlemen staring at them from the orchestra. But *les honnétes gens* of every class are largely represented, and it is clear that even people of serious tastes look upon the theatre not as one of the "extras," but as one of the necessities, of life—a periodical necessity hardly less frequent and urgent than their evening paper and their *demi-tasse*. I am always struck with the number of elderly men, decorated, grizzled, and grave, for whom the stage has kept its mysteries. You may see them at the Palais Royal, listening complacently to the carnival of *grivoiseries* nightly enacted there, and at the *Variétés*, levelling their glasses paternally at the lightly-clad heroines of Offenbach. The truth is that in the theatre the French mind *se reconnait*, according to its own idiom, more vividly than elsewhere. Its supreme faculty, the art of form, of arrangement and presentation, is preeminently effective on the stage, and I suppose many a good citizen has before this consoled himself for his country's woes by reflecting that if the Germans *have* a Gravelotte in their records, they have not a "Rabagas," and if they possess a Bismarck and a Moltke, they have neither a Dumas *fils* nor a Schneider. A good French play is an admirable work of art, of which it behooves patrons of the contemporary English drama, at any rate, to speak with respect. It serves its purpose to perfection, and French dramatists, as far as I can see, have no more secrets to learn. The first half-dozen a foreign spectator listens to seem to him among the choicest productions of the human mind, and it is only little by little that he becomes conscious of the extraordinary meagreness of their material. The *substance* of the plays I have lately seen seems to me, when I think them over, something really amazing, and it is what I had chiefly in mind in speaking just now of the stage as an index of social character. Prime material was evidently long ago exhausted, and the best that can be done now is to rearrange old situations with a kind of desperate ingenuity. The field looks terribly narrow, but it is still cleverly worked. "An old theme—but with a difference," the workman claims; and he makes the most of his difference—for laughter if he is an *amateur* pure and simple; for tears, if he is a moralist.

Do not for a moment imagine that moralists are wanting. Alexandre Dumas *fils* is one—he is a dozen, indeed, in his single self. M. Pailleron (whose "Hélène" is the last novelty at the Théâtre Français) is another; and I am not sure that, since "Rabagas," M. Sardou is not a third. The great dogma of M. Dumas *fils* is, that if your wife is persistently unfaithful to you, you must kill her. He leaves you, I suppose, the choice of weapons; but that the thing must somehow be done, he has written a famous pamphlet, now reaching its fortieth edition, to prove. M. Pailleron holds, on the other hand, that if it was before your marriage, and before she had ever heard of you, and with her cousin, when she was a child and knew no better, you must— after terrific vituperation, indeed, and imminent suicide on the lady's part—press her relentlessly to your bosom. M. Pailleron enforces this moral in capitally turned verse, and with Delaunay's magical aid; but as I sat through his piece the other evening, I racked my brain to discover what heinous offence Delicacy has ever committed that she should have to do such cruel penance. I am afraid that she has worse things in store for her, for the event of the winter (if a *coup d'état* does not carry off the honors) is to be the new play of Dumas *fils*, "La Femme de Claude." Whatever becomes of the state, I shall go early to see the play, for it is to have the services of the first actress in the world. I have not the smallest hesitation in so qualifying Mademoiselle Desclée. She has just been sustaining by her sole strength the weight of a ponderous drama called "La Gueule du Loup," in which her acting seemed to me a revelation of the capacity of the art. I have never seen nature grasped so in its essence, and rendered with a more amazing mastery of the fine shades of expression. Just as the light drama in France is a tissue of fantastic indecencies, the serious drama is an agglomeration of horrors. I had supped so full of these that, before seeing the "Gueule du Loup," I had quite made up my mind to regard as an offence against civilization every new piece, whether light or serious, of which the main idea should not be *pleasing*. To do anything so pleasant as to please is the last thing that M. Dumas and his school think of. But Mlle. Desclée renders the chief situation of M. Laya's drama—that of a woman who has fancied herself not as other women are, coming to her senses at the bottom of a moral abyss, and measuring the length of her fall— with a verity so penetrating that I could not but ask myself whether, to become a wholesome and grateful spectacle, even the ugliest possibilities of life need anything more than rigorous exactness of presentation. Mlle. Desclée, at any rate, was for half-an-hour the most powerful of moralists. M. Laya, her author, on the other hand, is an atrocious one. His trivial *dénoue-ment*, treading on the heels of the sombre episode I have mentioned, is an insult to the spectator's sympathies. Even Mlle. Desclée's acting fails to give it dignity. Here, as every-where, an inexpressible want of moral intelligence is the strik-ing point. Novel and drama alike betray an incredibly superficial perception of the moral side of life. It is not only that adultery is their only theme, but that the treatment of it is so monstrously vicious and arid. It has been used now for so many years as a mere pigment, a source of dramatic color, a *ficelle*, as they say, that it has ceased to have any apparent moral bearings. It is turned inside out by hungering poetasters in search of a new "effect" as freely as an old glove by some thrifty dame intent on placing a prudent stitch. I might cite some striking examples, if I had space; some are too detestable. I do not know that I have found anything more suggestive than the revival, at the Gymnase, of that too familiar drama of the younger (the then very youthful) Dumas, the "Dame aux Camélias." Mlle. Pierson plays the heroine—Mlle. Pierson the history of whose *embon-point* is one of the topics of the day. She was formerly almost corpulent—fatally so for that beauty which even her rivals ad-mitted to be greater than her talent. She devoted herself bravely to a diet of raw meat and other delicacies recommended by Ban-ting, and she has recently emerged from the ordeal in sylphlike slenderness. This result, I believe, "draws" powerfully, though it seemed to me, I confess, that even raw meat had not made Mlle. Pierson an actress. I went to the play because I had read in the weekly *feuilleton* of that very sound and sensible critic, M. Francisque Sarcey, that even in its old age it bore itself like a masterpiece, and produced an immense effect. If I could speak with the authority of Dr. Johnson, I should be tempted to qualify it with that vigorous brevity which he sometimes used so well. In the *entr'actes* I took refuge in the street to laugh at my ease over its colossal flimsiness. But I should be sorry to linger on the sombre side of the question, and my intention, indeed, was to make a note of none but pleasant impressions. I have, after all, received so many of these in Paris play-houses that my stricture seems gracelessly cynical. I bear the actors, at least, no grudge; they are better than the authors. Molière and De Musset, moreover, have not yet lost favor, and Corneille's "Cid" was recently revived with splendor and success. Here is a store of imperishable examples. What I shall think of regretfully when I have parted with the opportunity is not the *tragedies bourgeoises* of MM. Dumas, Feuillet, and Pailleron, but the inimitable Got strutting about as the *podestà* in the "Caprices de Marianne," and twitching his magisterial train from the nerveless grasp of that delicious idiot, his valet; and Delaunay murmuring his love notes like a summer breeze in the ear of the blonde Cécile, and Coquelin as *Mascarille*, looking like an old Venetian print, and playing as if the author of the "Etourdi" were in the *coulisse*, prompting him; and M. Mannet-Sully (the ardent young *débutant* of the "Cid") shouting with the most picturesque fury possible the famous sortie:

"Paraissez Navarrins, Maures, Castillans!"

To an ingenuous American the Théâtre Français may yet offer an aesthetic education.

A EUROPEAN SUMMER:
FROM VENICE TO STRASSBURG
March 1873

Bridge of Sighs, Venice, ca. 1850.

THERE WOULD BE MUCH TO SAY ABOUT THAT GOLDEN CHAIN
of historic cities which stretches from Milan to Venice, in
which the very names—Brescia, Verona, Mantua, Padua—are
an ornament to one's phrase; but I should have to draw upon
recollections now three years old, and to make my short story a

long one. Of Verona and Venice only have I recent impressions, and even to these I must do hasty justice. I came into Venice, just as I had done before, toward the end of a summer's day, when the shadows begin to lengthen, and the light to glow, and found that the attendant sensations bore repetition remarkably well. There was the same last intolerable delay at Mestre, just before your first glimpse of the lagoon confirms the already distinct sea-smell which has added speed to the precursive flight of your imagination; then the liquid level, edged far off by its band of undiscriminated domes and spires, soon distinguished and proclaimed, however, as excited and contentious heads multiply at the windows of the train; then your long rumble on the immense white railway bridge, which, in spite of the invidious contrast drawn (very properly) by Mr. Ruskin, between the old and the new approach to Venice, does truly, in a manner, shine across the green lap of the lagoon like a mighty causeway of marble; then the plunge into the station, which would be exactly similar to every other plunge, save for one little fact—that the key-note of the great medley of voices borne back from the exit is not "Cab, sir!" but "Barca, signore!" I don't mean, however, to follow the traveller through every phase of his initiation, at the risk of stamping poor Venice beyond repair as the supreme bugbear of literature; though, for my own part, I hold that, to a fine, healthy appetite for the picturesque, the subject cannot be too diffusely treated. Meeting on the Piazza, on the evening of my arrival, a young American painter, who told me that he had been spending the summer at Venice, I could have assaulted him, for very envy. He was painting, forsooth, the interior of Saint Mark's. To be a young American painter unperplexed by the mocking, elusive soul of things, and satisfied with their wholesome, light-bathed surface and shape; keen of eye; fond of color, of sea and sky, and anything that may chance between them; of old lace, and old brocade, and old furniture (even when made to order); of time-mellowed harmonies on nameless canvases, and happy contours in cheap old engravings; to spend one's mornings in still, productive analysis of the clustered shadows of the Basilica, one's afternoons anywhere, in church or camp, on canal or lagoon, and one's evenings in starlight gossip at Florian's, feeling the sea-breeze throb languidly between the two great pillars of the Piazzetta and over the low, black domes of the church—this, I consider, is to be as happy as one may safely be.

The mere use of one's eyes, in Venice, is happiness enough, and generous observers find it hard to keep an account of their profits in this line. Everything the eye rests on is effective, pictorial, harmonious—thanks to some inscrutable flattery of the atmosphere. Your brown-skinned, white-shirted gondolier, twisting himself in the light, seems to you, as you lie staring beneath your awning, a perpetual symbol of Venetian "effect." The light here is, in fact, a mighty magician, and, with all respect to

Titian, Veronese, and Tintoret, the greatest artist of them all. You should see, in places, the material on which it works—slimy brick, marble battered and befouled, rags, dirt, decay. Sea and sky seem to meet halfway, to blend their tones into a kind of soft iridescence, a lustrous compound of wave and cloud, and a hundred nameless local reflections, and then to fling the clear tissue against every object of vision. You may see these elements at work everywhere, but to see them in their intensity you should choose the finest day of the month, and have yourself rowed far away across the lagoon to Torcello. Without making this excursion, you can hardly pretend to know Venice, or to sympathize with that longing for pure radiance which animated her great colorists. It is a perfect bath of light, and I could not get rid of a fancy that we were cleaving the upper atmosphere on some hurrying cloud-skiff. At Torcello there is nothing but the light to see—nothing, at least, but a sort of blooming sand-bar, intersected by a single narrow creek which does duty as a canal, and occupied by a meagre cluster of huts, the dwellings, apparently, of market-gardeners and fishermen, and by a ruinous church of the eleventh century. It is impossible to imagine a more poignant embodiment of unheeded decline. Torcello was the mother-city of Venice, and it lies there now, a mere mouldering vestige, like a group of weather-bleached parental bones left impiously unburied. I stopped my gondola at the mouth of the shallow inlet, and walked along the grass beside a hedge to the low-browed, crumbling Cathedral. The charm of certain vacant grassy spaces, in Italy, overfrowned by masses of brickwork, honeycombed by the suns of centuries, is something that I hereby renounce, once for all, the attempt to express; but you may be sure, whenever I mention such a spot, that it is something delicious. A delicious stillness covered the little campo at Torcello; I remember none so *audible* save that of the Roman Campagna. There was no life there but the visible tremor of the brilliant air and the cries of half-a-dozen young children, who dogged our steps and clamored for coppers. These children, by the way, were the handsomest little brats in the world, and each was furnished with a pair of eyes which seemed a sort of protest of nature against the stinginess of fortune. They were very nearly as naked as savages, and their little bellies protruded like those of infant Abyssinians in the illustrations of books of travel; but as they scampered and sprawled in the soft, thick grass, grinning like suddenly translated cherubs, and showing their hungry little teeth, they suggested forcibly that the best assurance of happiness in this world is to be found in the maximum of innocence and the minimum of wealth. One small urchin—framed, if ever a child was, to be the joy of an aristocratic mamma—was the most expressively beautiful little mortal I ever looked upon. He had a smile to make Correggio sigh in his grave; and yet here he was, running wild among these sea-stunted bushes, on the lovely margin of a decaying world, in prelude to how blank, or to how dark, a destiny? Verily, nature is still at odds with fortune; though, indeed, if they ever really pull together, I'm afraid nature will lose her picturesqueness. An infant citizen of our own republic, straight-haired, pale-eyed, and freckled, duly darned and catechised, marching into a New England school-house, is an object often seen and soon forgotten; but I think I shall always remember, with infinite tender conjecture, as the years roll by, this little unlettered Eros of the Adriatic strand. Yet all youthful things at Torcello were not cheerful, for the poor lad who brought us the key of the Cathedral was shaking with an ague, and his melancholy presence seemed to point the moral of forsaken nave and choir. The church is admirably primitive and curious, and reminded me of the two or three oldest churches of Rome—St. Clement and St. Agnes. The interior is rich in grimly mystical mosaics of the twelfth century, and the patchwork of precious fragments in the pavement is not inferior to that of St. Mark's. But the terribly distinct apostles are ranged against their dead gold backgrounds as stiffly as grenadiers presenting arms—intensely personal sentinels of a personal Deity. Their stony stare seems to wait for ever vainly for some visible revival of primitive orthodoxy, and one may well wonder whether it finds much beguilement in idly-gazing troops of Western heretics—passionless, even in their heresy.

I had been curious to see whether, in the galleries and churches of Venice, I should be disposed to transpose my old estimates—to burn what I had adored, and to adore what I had burned. It is a sad truth, that one can stand in the Ducal Palace for the first time but once, with the deliciously ponderous sense of that particular half-hour being an èra in one's mental history; but I had the satisfaction of finding at least a great comfort in a short stay—that none of my early memories were likely to change places, and that I could take up my admirations where I had left them. I still found Carpaccio delightful, Veronese magnificent, Titian supremely beautiful, and Tintoret altogether unqualifiable. I repaired immediately to the little church of San Cassano, which contains the smaller of Tintoret's two great Crucifixions, and when I had looked at it awhile, I drew a long breath, and felt that I could contemplate any other picture in Venice with proper self-possession. It seemed to me that I had advanced to the uttermost limit of painting; that beyond that another art—inspired poetry—begins, and that Bellini, Veronese, Giorgione, and Titian, all joining hands and straining every muscle of their genius, reach forward not so far but that they leave a visible space, in which Tintoret alone is master. I well remember the excitement into which he plunged me, when I first learned to know him; but the glow of that comparatively youthful amazement is dead, and with it, I fear, that confident vivacity of phrase of which, in trying to utter my impressions, I felt less the magniloquence than the impotence. In his power there are many weak spots, mysterious lapses, and fitful intermissions; but, when the list of his faults is complete, he still seems to me to remain the most *interesting* of painters. His reputation rests chiefly on a more superficial sort of merit— his energy, his unsurpassed productivity, his being, as Théophile Gautier says, *le roi des fougueux*. These qualities are immense, but the great source of his impressiveness is that his indefatigable hand never drew a line that was not, as one may say, a moral line. No painter ever had such breadth and such depth; and even Titian, beside him, has often seemed to me but a great decorative artist. Mr. Ruskin, whose eloquence, in dealing with the great Venetians, sometimes outruns his discretion, is fond of speaking even of Veronese as a painter of deep spiritual intentions. This, it seems to me, is pushing matters too far, and the author of the "Rape of Europa" is, pictorially speaking, no greater casuist than any other genius of supreme good taste. Titian was, assuredly, a mighty poet, but Tintoret—Tintoret was almost a prophet. Before his greatest works you are conscious of a sudden evaporation of old doubts and dilemmas, and the eternal problem of the conflict between idealism and realism dies the most natural of deaths. In Tintoret, the problem is practically solved, and the alternatives so harmoniously interfused that I defy the keenest critic to say where one begins and the other ends. The homeliest prose melts into the most ethereal poetry, and the literal and imaginative fairly confound their identity. This, however, is vague praise. Tintoret's great merit, to my mind, was his unequalled distinctness of vision. When once he had conceived the germ of a scene, it defined itself to his imagination with an intensity, an amplitude, an individuality of expression, which make one's observation of his pictures seem less an operation of the mind than a kind of supplementary experience of life. Veronese and Titian are content with a much looser specification, as their treatment of any subject which Tintoret has also treated abundantly proves. There are few more suggestive contrasts than that between the absence of a *total* character at all commensurate with its scattered variety and brilliancy, in Veronese's "Marriage of Cana," in the Louvre, and the poignant, almost startling, completeness of Tintoret's illustration of the theme, at the Salute Church. To compare his "Presentation of the Virgin," at the Madonna dell' Orto, with Titian's, at the Academy, or his "Annunciation" with Titian's, close at hand, is to measure the essential difference between observation and imagination. One has certainly not said all that there is to say for Titian when one has called him an observer. *Il y mettait du sien*, as the French say, and I use the term to designate roughly the artist whose apprehensions, infinitely deep and strong when applied to the single figure or to easily-balanced groups, spends itself vainly on great dramatic combinations— or, rather, leaves them ungauged. It was the whole scene that Tintoret seemed to have beheld, in a flash of inspiration intense enough to stamp it ineffaceably on his perceptions; and it was the whole scene, complete, peculiar, individual, unprecedented, which he committed to canvas with all the vehemence of his talent. Compare his "Last Supper," at San Giorgio—its long, diagonally-placed table, its dusky spaciousness, its scattered lamp-light and halo-light, its startled, gesticulating figures, its richly realistic foreground—with the usual formal, almost mathematical, rendering of the subject, in which impressiveness seems to have been sought in elimination rather than comprehension. You get from Tintoret's work the impression that he *felt*, pictorially, the great, beautiful, terrible spectacle of human life very much as Shakespeare felt it poetically—with a heart that never ceased to beat a passionate accompaniment to every stroke of his brush. Thanks to this fact, his works are signally grave, and their almost universal and rapidly increasing decay does not relieve their gloom. Nothing, indeed, can well be sadder than the great collection of Tintorets at San Rocco. Incurable blackness is settling fast upon all of them, and they frown at you across the sombre splendor of their great chambers like gaunt, twilight phantoms of pictures. To our children's children, Tintoret, as things are going, can be hardly more than a name; and such of them as shall miss the tragic beauty, already so dimmed and stained, of the great "Bearing of the Cross," at San Rocco, will live and die without knowing the largest eloquence of art. If you wish to add the last touch of solemnity to the place, recall, as vividly as possible, while you linger at San

Rocco, the painter's singularly interesting portrait of himself, at the Louvre. The old man looks out of the canvas from beneath a brow as sad as a sunless twilight, with just such a stoical hopelessness as you might fancy him to wear, if he stood at your side, gazing at his rotting canvases. It is not whimsical to fancy it the face of a man who felt that he had given the world more than the world was likely to repay. Indeed, before every picture of Tintoret, you may remember this tremendous portrait with profit. On one side, the power, the passion, the illusion of his art; on the other, the mortal fatigue of his spirit. The world's knowledge of Tintoret is so small that the portrait throws a doubly precious light on his personality; and when we wonder vainly what manner of man he was, and what were his purpose, his faith, and his method, we may find forcible assurance there that they were, at any rate, his life—and a very intense one.

Verona, which was my last Italian stopping-place, is under any circumstances a delightfully interesting city; but the kindness of my own memory of it is deepened by a subsequent ten days' experience of Germany. I rose one morning at Verona, and went to bed at night at Botzen! The statement needs no comment, and the two places, though but fifty miles apart, are as painfully dissimilar as their names. I had prepared myself for your delectation with a copious tirade on German manners, German scenery, German art, and the German stage—on the lights and shadows of Innsbruck, Munich, Nuremberg, and

Heidelberg; but just as I was about to put pen to paper, I glanced into a little volume on these very topics, lately published by that famous novelist and moralist, M. Ernest Feydeau, the fruit of a summer's observation at Hamburg. This work produced a reaction, and if I chose to follow M. Feydeau's own example when he wishes to qualify his approbation, I might call his treatise by any vile name known to the speech of man, but I content myself with pronouncing it—superficial. I then reflect that my own opportunities for seeing and judging were extremely limited, and I suppress my tirade, lest some more enlightened critic should come and pronounce *me* superficial. Its sum and substance was to have been that—superficially—Germany is ugly; that Munich is a nightmare, Heidelberg a disappointment (in spite of its charming Castle), and even Nuremberg not a joy for ever. But comparisons are odious; and if Munich is ugly, Verona is beautiful enough. You may laugh at my logic, but you will probably assent to my meaning. I carried away from Verona a certain mental picture upon which I cast an introspective glance whenever between Botzen and Strassburg the oppression of external circumstance became painful. It was a lovely August afternoon in the Roman Arena—a ruin in which repair and restoration have been so gradually and discreetly practised that it seems all of one harmonious antiquity. The vast stony oval rose high against the sky in a single, clear, continuous line, broken here and there only by strolling and reclining loungers. The massive tiers inclined in solid monotony to the central circle, in which a small open-air theatre was in active operation. A small section of the great slope of masonry facing the stage was roped off into an auditorium, in which the narrow level space between the footlights and the lowest step figured as the pit. Footlights are a figure of speech, for the performance was going on in the broad glow of the afternoon, with a delightful, and apparently by no means misplaced, confidence in the good-will of the spectators. What the piece was that was deemed so superbly able to shift for itself I know not—very possibly the same drama that I remember seeing advertised during my former visit to Verona—nothing less than *La Tremenda Giustizia di Dio*. If titles are worth anything this product of the melodramatist's art might surely stand upon its own legs. Along the tiers above the little group of regular spectators was gathered a sort of free-list of unauthorized observers, who although beyond ear-shot must have been enabled by the generous breadth of Italian gesture to follow the tangled thread of the piece. It was all deliciously Italian—the mixture of old life and new, the mountebank's booth (it was hardly more) grafted upon the antique circus, the dominant presence of a mighty architecture, the loungers and idlers beneath the kindly sky, upon the sun-warmed stones. I never felt more keenly the difference between the background to life in the Old World and the New. There are other things in Verona to make it a liberal education to be born there—though that it is one for the contemporary Veronese, I don't pretend to say. The Tombs of the Scaligers, with their soaring pinnacles, their high-poised canopies, their exquisite refinement and concentration of the Gothic idea, I cannot profess, even after much worshipful gazing, to have fully comprehended and enjoyed. They seemed to me full of deep architectural meanings, such as must drop gently into the mind, one by one, after infinite tranquil contemplation. But even to the hurried and preoccupied traveller the solemn little chapel-yard in the city's heart, in which they stand girdled by their great swaying curtain of linked and twisted iron, is one of the most impressive spots in Italy. Nowhere else is such a wealth of artistic achievement crowded into so narrow a space; nowhere else are the daily comings and goings of men blessed by the presence of *manlier* art. Verona is rich, furthermore, in beautiful churches—several with beautiful names: San Fermo, Santa Anastasia, San Zenone. This last is a structure of high antiquity, and of the most impressive loveliness. The nave terminates in a double choir—that is, a sub-choir or crypt, into which you descend, and wander among primitive columns whose variously grotesque capitals rise hardly higher than your head, and an upper choral level into which you mount by broad stairways of the most picturesque effect. I shall never forget the impression of majestic chastity that I received from the great nave of the building on my former visit. I decided to my satisfaction then that every church is from the devotional point of view a solecism that has not something of a similar absolute felicity of proportion; for strictly formal beauty seems best to express our conception of spiritual beauty. The nobly serious effect of San Zenone is deepened by its single picture—a masterpiece of the most serious of painters, the severe and exquisite Mantegna.

THE AFTER-SEASON AT ROME
May 20, 1873

The Spanish Steps, ca. 1908.

ONE MAY SAY WITHOUT INJUSTICE TO ANY BODY THAT THE state of mind of a great many foreigners in Rome is one of intense impatience for the moment when all other foreigners shall have departed. One may confess to this state of mind, and be no misanthrope. Rome has passed so completely for the winter months into the hands of the barbarians that that estimable

character, the "quiet observer," finds it constantly harder to con-
centrate his attention. He has an irritating sense of his impressions being perverted and adulterated; the venerable visage of
Rome betrays an unbecoming eagerness to see itself mirrored in
English, American, German eyes. It is not simply that you are
never first or never alone at the classic or historic spots where
you have dreamt of persuading the shy *genius loci* into confidential utterance; it is not simply that St. Peter's, the Vatican, the
Palatine, are for ever ringing with English voices: it is the general oppressive feeling that the city of the soul has become for
the time a monstrous mixture of the watering-place and the
curiosity-shop, and that its most ardent life is that of the tourists
who haggle over false intaglios, and yawn through palaces and
temples. But you are told of a happy time when these abuses begin to pass away, when Rome becomes Rome again, and you
may have it all to yourself. "You may like Rome more or less
now," I was told during the height of the season; "but you must
wait till the month of May to love it. Then the foreigners, or the
excess of them, are gone; the galleries and ruins are empty, and
the place," said my informant, who was a Frenchman, "*renaît à
elle-méme*," Indeed, I was haunted all winter by an irresistible
prevision of what Rome *must* be in spring. Certain charming
places seemed to murmur: "Ah, this is nothing! Come back in
May, and see the sky above us almost black with its excess of
blue, and the new grass already deep, but still vivid, and the

148

white roses tumbling in odorous spray over the walls, and the warm radiant air dropping gold into all our coloring."

A month ago I spent a week in the country, and on my return, the first time I went into the Corso, I became conscious of a change. Something very pleasant had happened, but at first I was at a loss to define it. Then suddenly I comprehended—there were but half as many people, and these were chiefly good Italians. There had been a great exodus, and now, physically, morally, aesthetically, there was elbow-room. In the afternoon I went to the Pincio, and the Pincio was almost dull. The band was playing to a dozen ladies, as they lay in their landaus, poising their lace-fringed parasols; but they had only one light-gloved dandy apiece hanging over their carriage-doors. By the parapet of the great terrace which sweeps the city stood three or four quiet observers looking at the sunset, with their Baedekers peeping out of their pockets; the sunsets not being down with their tariff in these precious volumes, I good-naturedly hoped that, like myself, they were committing the harmless folly of taking mental possession of the scene before them.

It is the same good-nature that leads me to violate the instinct of monopoly, and proclaim that Rome in May is worth waiting for. I have just been so gratified at finding myself in undisturbed possession for a couple of hours of the Museum of the Lateran that I can afford to be magnanimous. And yet I keep within the bounds of reason when I say that it would be hard as a traveller or student to pass pleasanter days than these. The weather for a month has been perfect, the sky magnificently blue, the air lively enough, the nights cool, too cool, and the whole gray old city illumined with the most irresistible smile. Rome, which in some moods, especially to new-comers, seems a terribly gloomy place, gives on the whole, and as one knows it better, an indefinable impression of gaiety. This contagious influence lurks in all its darkness and dirt and decay—a something more careless and hopeless than our thrifty Northern cheerfulness, and yet more genial, more urbane, than mere indifference. The Roman temper is a healthy and happy one, and you feel it abroad in the streets even when the *scirocco* blows, and the goal of man's life assumes a horrible identity with the mouth of a furnace. But who can analyze even the simplest Roman impression? It is compounded of so many things, it says so much, it suggests so much, it so quickens the intellect and so flatters the heart, that before we are fairly conscious of it the imagination has marked it for her own, and exposed us to a perilous likelihood of talking nonsense about it.

The smile of Rome, as I have called it, and its intense suggestiveness to those who are willing to ramble irresponsibly and take things as they come, is ushered in with the first breath of spring, and it grows and grows with the advancing season, till it wraps the whole place in its tenfold charm. As the process goes on, you can do few better things than go often to the Villa Bor-

ghese, and sit on the grass (on a stout bit of drapery) and watch
its exquisite stages. It is a more magical spring than ours, even
when ours has left off its damnable faces, and begun. Nature sur-
renders herself to it with a frankness which outstrips your most
unutterable longings, and leaves you, as I say, nothing to do but
to lay your head among the anemones at the base of a high-
stemmed pine, and gaze up crestward and skyward along its slanting silvery column. You may look at the spring in Rome from a
dozen of these choice standpoints, and have a different villa for
your observations every day in the week. The Doria, the Ludovisi, the Medici, the Albani, the Wolkonski, the Chigi, the Mel-
lini, the Massimo—there are more of them, with all their sights,
and sounds, and odors, and memories, than you have senses for.
But I prefer none of them to the Borghese, which is free to all the
world at all times, and yet never crowded; for when the whirl of
carriages is great in the middle regions, you may find a hundred
untrodden spots and silent corners, tenanted at the worst by a
group of those long-skirted young Propagandists, who stalk about
with solemn angularity, each with a book under his arm, like sil-
houettes from a mediaeval missal, and "compose" so extremely
well with the picturesqueness of cypresses, and of stretches of
golden-russet wall overtopped by the intense blue sky. And yet if
the Borghese is good, the Medici is strangely charming; and you
may stand in the little belvedere which rises with such surpassing
oddity out of the dusky heart of the Boschetto at the latter

establishment—a miniature presentation of the wand of the Sleeping Beauty—and look across at the Ludovisi pines lifting their crooked parasols into a sky of what a painter would call the most *morbid* blue, and declare that the place where they grew is the most delightful in the world. The Villa Ludovisi has been all winter the residence of the lady familiarly known in Roman society as "Rosina," the king's morganatic wife. But this, apparently, is the only familiarity which she allows, for the grounds of the villa have been rigidly closed, to the inconsolable regret of old Roman sojourners. But just as the nightingales began to sing, the august *padrona* departed, and the public, with certain restrictions, have been admitted to hear them. It is a really princely place, and there could be no better example of the expansive tendencies of ancient privilege than the fact of its whole vast extent falling within the city walls. It has in this respect very much the same sort of impressiveness as the great intramural demesne of Magdalen College at Oxford. The stern old ramparts of Rome form the outer enclosure of the villa, and hence a series of picturesque effects which it would be unscrupulous flattery to say you can imagine. The grounds are laid out in the formal last-century manner; but nowhere do the straight black cypresses lead off the gaze into vistas of a more fictive sort of melancholy; nowhere are there grander, smoother walls of laurel and myrtle.

I recently spent an afternoon hour at the little Protestant cemetery close to St. Paul's Gate, where the ancient and the

modern world are most impressively contrasted. They make between them one of the solemn places of Rome—although, indeed, when funereal things are so interfused with picturesqueness,
it seems ungrateful to call them sad. Here is a mixture of tears
and smiles, of stones and flowers, of mourning cypresses and radiant sky, which almost tempts one to fancy one is looking back
at death from the brighter side of the grave. The cemetery nes-
tles in an angle of the city wall, and the older graves are sheltered by a mass of ancient brickwork, through whose narrow
loopholes you may peep at the purple landscape of the Campagna. Shelley's grave is here, buried in roses—a happy grave
every way for a poet who was personally poetic. It is impossible
to imagine anything more impenetrably tranquil than this little
corner in the bend of the protecting rampart. You seem to see a
cluster of modern ashes held tenderly in the rugged hand of the
Past. The past is tremendously embodied in the hoary pyramid
of Caius Cestius, which rises hard by, half within the wall and
half without, cutting solidly into the solid blue of the sky, and
casting its pagan shadow upon the grass of English graves—that
of Keats, among others—with a certain poetic justice. It is a
wonderful confusion of mortality and a grim enough admonition
of our helpless promiscuity in the crucible of time. But to my
sense, the most touching thing there is the look of the pious
English inscriptions among all these Roman memories. There
is something extremely appealing in their universal expression

of that worst of trouble—trouble in a foreign land; but something that stirs the heart even more deeply is the fine Scriptural language in which everything is recorded. The echoes of massive Latinity with which the atmosphere is charged suggest nothing more majestic and monumental. I may seem unduly sentimental; but I confess that the charge to the reader in the monument to Miss Bathurst, who was drowned in the Tiber in 1824: "If thou art young and lovely, build not thereon, for she who lies beneath thy feet in death was the loveliest flower ever crept in its bloom"—seemed to me irresistibly a case for tears. The whole elaborate inscription, indeed, was curiously suggestive. The English have the reputation of being the most reticent people in the world, and, as there is no smoke without fire, I suppose they have done something to deserve it; but for my own part, I am for ever meeting the most startling examples of the insular faculty to "gush." In this instance the mother of the deceased takes the public into her confidence with surprising frankness, omits no detail, and embraces the opportunity to mention by the way that she had already lost her husband by a most mysterious death. Yet the whole elaborate record is profoundly touching. It has an air of old-fashioned gentility which makes its frankness tragic. You seem to hear the garrulity of passionate grief.

To be choosing this well-worn picturesqueness for a theme, when there are matters of modern moment going on in Rome, may seem to demand some apology. But I can make no claim to your special correspondent's faculty for getting an "inside view" of things, and I have hardly more than a picturesque impression of the Pope's illness and of the discussion of the Law of the Convents. Indeed, I am afraid to speak of the Pope's illness at all, lest I should say something egregiously heartless about it, and recall too forcibly that unnatural husband who was heard to wish that his wife would get well or—something! He had his reasons, and Roman tourists have theirs in the shape of a vague hankering for something spectacular at St. Peter's. If it takes a funeral to produce it, a funeral let it be. Meanwhile, we have been having a glimpse of the spectacular side of the Religious Corporations Act. Hearing one morning a great hubbub in the Corso, I stepped forth upon my balcony. A couple of hundred men were strolling slowly down the street with their hands in their pockets, shouting in unison, "*Abbasso il ministero!*" and huzzaing in chorus. Just beneath my window they stopped and began to murmur, "*Al Quirinale, al Quirinale!*" The crowd surged a moment gently, and then drifted to the Quirinal, where it scuffled harmlessly with half a dozen of the king's soldiers. It ought to have been impressive, for what was it essentially but the seeds of revolution? But its carriage was too gentle and its cries too musical to send the most timorous tourist to packing his trunk. As I began with saying: in Rome, in May, everything has an amiable side, even *émeutes!*

HOMBURG REFORMED

July 28, 1873

Bad Homburg Palace, ca. 1860.

I HAVE BEEN FINDING HOMBURG A VERY PLEASANT PLACE, but have been half ashamed to confess it. People assure me on all sides that its glory is sadly dimmed, and that it can only be rightly enjoyed to the music of *roulette* and of clinking napoleons. It is known by this time, I suppose, even in those virtuously disinterested communities where these lines may circulate, that the day of *roulette* in these regions is over, and that in the matter of *rouge-et-noir* united Germany has taken a new departure. The last unhallowed gains at the green tables were pocketed last summer, and the last hard losses, doubtless, as imperturbably endured as if good-natured chance had still a career to run. Chance, I believe, at Homburg was not amazingly good-natured, and kept her choicest favors for the bank; but now that the reign of Virtue has begun, I have no doubt there are plenty of irregular characters who think that she was much the more amiable creature of the two. What provision has been made for this adventurous multitude I am at loss to conceive, and how life strikes people now for whom, at any time these twenty years, it has been concentrated in the shifting victory of red or black. Some of them have taken to better courses, I suppose; some of them, doubtless, to worse; but I have a notion that many of them have begun to wear away the dull remainder of existence in a kind of melancholy, ghostly hovering around the deserted Kursaals. I have seen many of these blighted survivors sitting about under the trees in the Kurgarten, with the old habit of imperturbability still in their blank, fixed faces—neat, elderly gentlemen, elderly ladies not especially venerable, whose natural attitude seems to be to sit with their elbows on the table and their eyes on the game. They have all, of course, a pack of cards in their pockets, and their only consolation must be to play "patience" for evermore. When I remember, indeed, that I am in legendary Germany, I find it easy to believe that in these mild summer nights, when the stupid people who get up at six o'clock to drink the waters are safely in bed, they assemble in some far-away corner of the park, and make a green table of the moonlit grass. Twice a week the old gaming rooms at the Kursaal are thrown open, the chandeliers are lighted, and people go and stare at the painting and gilding. There is an immense deal of it, all in the elaborate rococo style in which French decorators of late years have become so proficient, and which makes an apartment look half like a throne-room and half like a café; but when you have walked about and looked at the undressed nymphs on the ceilings and the listless crowd in the great mirrors, you have nothing to do but to walk out again. The clever sumptuosity of the rooms makes virtue look rather foolish and dingy, and classes the famous M. Blanc, in the regard of pleasure-loving people, with the late Emperor of the French and other potentates more sinned against than sinning—martyred benefactors to that large portion of the human race who would fain consider the whole world as a watering-place. It is certainly hard to see what thrifty use the old gaming-rooms can be put to; they must stand there always in their gorgeous emptiness, like the painted tomb chambers of Eastern monarchs.

There was certainly fair entertainment in watching the play—and in playing, according to circumstances; but even in the old days I think I should have got my chief pleasure at the Kursaal in a spectacle which has survived the fall of M. Blanc. As you pass in the front door, you look straight across the breadth of the building through another great door which opens on the gardens. The Kursaal stands on an elevation, and the ground plunges away behind it with a great stretch, which spreads itself in a charming park. Beyond the park it rises again into the gentle slopes of the Taunus mountains, and makes a high wooded horizon. This picture of the green hollow and the blue ridge greets you as you come in, framed by the opposite doorway, and I have sometimes wondered whether in the gaming days an occasional novice with a tender conscience, on his way to the tables, may not have seemed to see in it the pleading face of that mild economist Mother Nature herself. It is, doubtless, thinking too fancifully of human nature to believe that a youth with a napoleon to stake, and the consciousness of no more rigid maternal presence than this, should especially heed the suggestion that it would be better far to take a walk in the woods. The truth is, I imagine, that Nature has no absolute voice, and that she speaks to us very much according to our moods. The view from the terrace at the Kursaal has often had confusion pronounced upon it by players with empty pockets, and has been sentimentally enjoyed by players with a run of luck. We have the advantage now, at least, of finding it always the same, and always extremely pretty. Homburg, indeed, is altogether a very pretty place, and its prettiness is of that pleasing sort which steals gradually on the attention. It is one of nature's own watering-places, and has no need, like so many of the audacious sisterhood, to bully you by force of fashion into thinking it tolerable.

Your half-hour's run from Frankfort across a great sunny expanse of corn-fields and crab-apple trees is indeed not particularly charming; but the sight of the town as you approach it, with its deep-red roofs rising out of thick shade at the base of its blue hills, is a pledge of salubrious repose. Homburg stands on a gentle spur of the highest of these hills, and one of its prettiest features is your seeing the line of level plain across the foot of its long sloping main street and the line of wooded mountain across the top. The main street, which is almost all of Homburg proper, has the look of busy idleness which belongs to watering-places. There are people strolling along and looking into the shop-windows who seem to be on the point of buying something for the sake of something to do. The shops deal chiefly in the lighter luxuries, and the young ladies who wait in them wear a great many ribbons and a great deal of hair. All the houses take lodgers, and every second one is a hotel, and every now and then you hear them chanting defiance at each other to the sound of the dinner-bell. In the middle of the street is the long red stuccoed façade of the Kursaal—the beating heart of the Homburg world, as one might have called it formerly. Its heart beats much slower now, but whatever social entertainment you may still find at Homburg you must look for there. People assemble there in very goodly crowds, if only to talk about the dreadful dulness and to commiserate each other for not having been here before. The place is kept up by a tax, promptly levied on all arriving strangers, and it seems to be prosperously enough maintained. It gives you a reading-room where you may go and practice indifference as you see a sturdy Briton settling down heavily over your coveted *Times*, just as you might of old when you saw the croupier raking in your stakes; music by a very fair band twice a day; a theatre, a café, a restaurant, and a table-d'hôte, and a garden illuminated every three or four evenings in the Vauxhall manner. People differ very much as to the satisfaction they take in sitting about under flaring gas-lamps and watching other people march up and down and pass and repass them by the hour. The pastime pushed to extremes tends, to my own thinking, to breed misanthropy—or an extra relish at least for a good book in one's own room and the path through the woods where one is least likely to meet any one. But if you use the Kursaal sparingly, and reserve it for an hour or two in the evening, it is certainly amusing enough.

I should be very sorry to underestimate the entertainment to be found in observing the comings and goings of a multifarious European crowd, or the number of suggestions and conclusions which, with a desultory logic of its own, the process contributes to one's philosophy of life. Every one who prefers to sit in a chair and look rather than walk up and down and be looked at, may be assumed to possess this intellectual treasure. The observations of the "cultivated American" bear chiefly, I think, upon the great topic of national idiosyncrasies. He is apt to have a keener sense of them than Europeans; it matters more to his imagination that his neighbor is English, French, or German. He often seems to me to be a creature wandering aloof, but half naturalized himself. His neighbors are outlined, defined, imprisoned, if you will, by their respective national moulds, pleasing or otherwise; but his own type has not hardened yet into the Old-World bronze. Superficially, no people carry more signs and tokens of what they are than Americans. I recognize them as they advance by the whole length of the promenade. The signs, however, are all of the negative kind, and seem to assure you, first of all, that the individual belongs to a country in which the social atmosphere, like the material, is extremely thin. American women, for the most part, in compliance with an instinct certainly not ungraceful, fill out the ideal mould with wonderful Paris dresses; but their dresses do little toward completing them, characterizing them, shelving and labelling them socially. The usual English lady, marching heavily about under the weight of her ingenious bad taste, has indescribably more the air of what one may call a social factor—the air of social responsibility, of having a part to play and a battle to fight. Sometimes, when the battle has been hard, the lady's face is very grim and unlovely, and I prefer the listless, rustling personality of my countrywomen; at others, when the cause has been graceful and the victory easy, she has a robust amenity which is one of the most agreeable things in the world. But these are metaphysical depths, though in strictness they ought not to be out of the way as one sits among German pipes and beer. The smokers and drinkers are the solid element at the Kursaal—the dominant tone is the German tone. It comes home very forcibly to the sense of our observant American, and it pervades, naturally enough, all his impressions of Homburg. People have come to feel strongly within the last four years that they must take the German tone into account, and they will find nothing here to lighten the task. If you have not been used to it, if you don't particularly relish it, you doubtless deserve some sympathy; but I advise you not to shirk it, to face it frankly as a superior critic would, and to call if necessary for a pipe and beer also, and build yourself into good humor with it. It is very pleasant, in an unfamiliar country, to collect travellers' evidence on local manners and national character. You are sure to have some vague impressions to be confirmed, some ingenious theory to be illustrated, some favorite prejudice in any case to be revived and improved. Even if your opportunities for observation are of the commonest kind, you find them serving your purpose. The smallest things become significant and eloquent, and demand a place in your note-book. I have learned no especial German secrets, I have penetrated into the bosom of no German families; but somehow I have received—I constantly receive—a weighty impression of Germany. It keeps me company as I walk in the woods and fields, and sits beside me—not precisely as a black care, but with an influence, as it were, which reminds one of the aftertaste of those articles of diet which you eat because they are good for you and not because you like them—when at last, of an evening, I have found the end of a bench on the promenade behind the Kursaal. One's impression of Germany may or may not be agreeable, but there is very little doubt that it is what one may call highly nutritive. In detail, it would take long to say what it consists of. I think that, in general, in such matters attentive observation confirms the common fame, and that you are very likely to find a people on your travels what you found them described to be under the mysterious wood-cut in some Peter Parley task-book or play-book of your child-hood. The French are a light, pleasure-loving people; ten years of the Boulevards brings no essential amendment to the phrase. The Germans are heavy and fair-haired, deep drinkers and strong thinkers; a fortnight at Homburg doesn't reverse the formula. The only thing to be said is that, as you grow older, French lightness and German weightiness become more complex ideas. A few weeks ago I left Italy in that really demoralized condition into which Italy throws those confiding spirits who give her unlimited leave to please them. Beauty, I had come to believe, was an ex-clusively Italian possession, the human face was not worth look-ing at unless redeemed by an Italian smile, nor the human voice worth listening to unless attuned to Italian vowels. A landscape was no landscape without vines festooned to fig-trees swaying in a hot wind—a mountain a hideous excrescence unless melting off into a Tuscan haze. But now that I have absolutely exchanged vines and figs for corn and cabbages, and violet Apennines for the homely plain of Frankfort, and liquids for gutturals, and the Italian smile for the German grin, I am much better contented than I could have ventured to expect. I have shifted my standard of beauty, but it still commands a glimpse of the divine idea.

There is something here, too, which pleases, suggests, and satisfies. Sitting of an evening in the Kurgarten, within ear-shot of the music, you have an almost inspiring feeling that you never have in Italy—a feeling that the substantial influences about you are an element of the mysterious future. They are of that varied order which seems to indicate the large needs of large natures. From its pavilion among the trees ring out the notes of the loud orchestra, playing Mozart, Beethoven, and Weber—such music as no other people has composed, as no other people can play it. Round about in close groups sit the sturdy, prosperous natives, with their capacious heads, their stout necks, their deep voices, their cigars, their beer, their intelligent applause, their talk on all things—largely enjoying, and yet strongly intending. Far away in the middle starlight stretch the dusky woods whose gentle murmur, we may suppose, unfolds here and there to a fanciful German ear some prophetic legend of a still larger success and a still richer Fatherland. The success of the Fatherland one sees reflected more or less vividly in all true German faces, and the relation between the face and the success seems demonstrated by a logic so unerring as to make envy vain. It is not the German success I envy, but the powerful German temperament and the comprehensive German brain. With these advantages one needn't be restless; one can afford to give a good deal of time to sitting out under the trees over pipes and beer and discussion tinged with metaphysics. But success of course is most forcibly embodied in the soldiers and officers who now form so large a proportion of every German group. You see them at all times lounging soberly about the gardens; you look at them (I do, at least) with a great deal of impartial deference, and you find in them something which seems a sort of pre-established negation of an adversary's chances. Compared with the shabby little unripe conscripts of France and Italy, they are indeed a solid brilliant phalanx. They are generally of excellent stature, and they have faces in which the look of education has not spoiled the look of good-natured simplicity. They are all equipped in brand new uniforms, and in these warm days they stroll about in spotless white trousers. Many of them wear their fine blonde beards, and they all look like perfect soldiers and excellent fellows. It doesn't do, of course, for an officer to seem too much like a good fellow, and the young captains and adjutants who ornament the Kurgarten of an evening seldom err in this direction. But they are business-like warriors to a man, and in their dark-blue uniforms and crimson facings, with their swords depending from their unbelted waists through a hole in their plain surtouts, they seem to suggest that war is somehow a better economy than peace.

But with all this, I am giving you Hamlet with Hamlet himself omitted. Though the gaming is stopped, the wells have not dried up, and people still drink them, and find them very good. They are indeed a very palatable dose, and "medical advice" at Homburg flatters one's egotism so unblushingly as rather to try the faith of people addicted to the old-fashioned confusion between the beneficial and the disagreeable. You have indeed to get up at half-past six o'clock—but of a fine summer morning this is no great hardship—and you are rewarded on your arrival at the spring by triumphant strains of music. There is an orchestra perched hard by, which plays operatic selections while you pace the shady walks and wait for your second glass. All the Homburg world is there; it's the fashionable hour; and at first I paid the antique prejudice just mentioned the tribute of thinking it was all too frivolous to be salutary. There are half a dozen springs, scattered through a charming wooded park, where you may find innumerable shady strolls and rustic benches in bosky nooks, where it is pleasant to lounge with a good light book. In the afternoon I drink at a spring with whose luxurious prettiness I still find it hard to associate a doctor's prescription. It reminds me of a back-scene at the theatre, and I feel as if I were drinking some fictitious draught prepared by the property-man; or rather, being a little white temple rising on slim columns among still green shade, it reminds me of some spot in the antique world where the goddess Hygeia was worshipped by thirsty pilgrims;

and I am disappointed to find that the respectable young woman who dips my glass is not a ministering nymph in a tunic and sandals. Beyond this valley of healing waters lie the great woods of fir and birch and beech and oak which cover the soft slopes of the Taunus. They are full of pleasant paths and of the frequent benches which testify to the German love of sitting in the open air. I don't know why it is—because, perhaps, we have all read so many Teutonic legends and ballads—but it comes natural in Germany to be in a wood. One need have no very rare culture, indeed, to find a vague old friendship in every feature of the landscape. The villages with their peaked roofs, covered with red scalloped shingles, and the brown beams making figures on the plastered cottage walls, the grape-vine on the wall, the swallows in the eaves, the Hausfrau, sickle in hand, with her yellow hair in a top-knot and her short blue skirt showing her black stockings—what is it all but a background to one of Richter's charming woodcuts? I never see a flock of geese on the roadside, and a little tow-pated maiden driving them with a forked switch, without thinking of Grimm's household tales. I look around for the old crone who is to come and inform her she is a king's daughter. I see nothing but the white Kaiserliche Deutsche sign-post, telling one that this is such and such a district of the Landwehr. But with such easy magic as this I am perhaps right in not especially regretting that the late enchantress of the Kursaal should have been handed over to the police.

AN EX-GRAND-DUCAL CAPITAL

September 6, 1873

Darmstadt Castle, Hessen, Germany, ca. 1900.

S PENDING THE SUMMER JUST PAST AT HOMBURG, I HAVE been conscious of a sort of gentle chronic irritation, of a natural sympathy with the whole race of suppressed, diminished, and mutilated sovereigns, in my frequent visits to the great dispeopled Schloss, about whose huge and awkward hulk the red roofs of the little town, as seen from a distance, cluster with an air of feudal allegiance, and which stands there as a respectable makeweight to the hardly scantier mass of the florid, fresh-colored Kursaal. It was formerly the appointed residence of the Landgrafs of the very diminutive state of Hesse-Homburg, the compact circumference of which these modest potentates might have the satisfaction of viewing, any fine morning, without a telescope, from their dressing-room windows. It is something of course to be monarch of a realm which slopes away with the slope of the globe into climates which it requires an effort to believe in and are part of the regular stock of geography; but perhaps we are apt to underestimate the peculiar complacency of a sovereign to whose possessions the blue horizon makes a liberal margin, and shows him his cherished inheritance visibly safe and sound, unclipped, unmenaced, shining like a jewel on its velvet cushion. This modest pleasure the Landgrafs of Hesse-Homburg must have enjoyed in perfection; the chronicle of their state-progresses should be put upon the same shelf as Xavier de Maistre's "*Voyage autour de ma Chambre.*" Though small, however, this rounded particle of sovereignty was still visible to the naked eye of diplomacy, and Herr von Bismarck, in 1866, swallowed it as smoothly as a gentleman following a tonic régime disposes of his homœopathic pellet. It had been merged shortly before in the neighboring empire of Hesse-Darmstadt, but promptly after Sadowa it was "ceded" to Prussia. Whoever is the loser, it has not been a certain lounging American on hot afternoons. The gates of the Schloss are now wide open, and the great garden is public property, and much resorted to by old gentlemen who dust off the benches with bandannas before sitting down, and by sheepish soldiers with affectionate sweethearts. Picturesquely, the palace is all it should be—very huge, very bare, very ugly, with great clean courts, in which round-barrelled Mecklenburg coach-horses must often have stood waiting for their lord and master to rise from table. The gateways are adorned with hideous sculptures of about 1650, representing wigged warriors on corpulent chargers, twisted pillars, and scroll-work like the "Flourishes" of a country writing-master—the whole glazed over with brilliant red paint. In the middle of the larger court stands an immense isolated round tower, painted white, and seen from all the country about. The gardens have very few flowers, and the sound of the rake nowadays is seldom heard on the gravel; but there are plenty of fine trees—some really stupendous poplars, untrimmed and spreading abroad like oaks, chestnuts which would make a figure in Italy, beeches which would be called "rather good" in England; plenty of nooks and bowers and densely-woven arcades, triumphs of old-fashioned gardenery; and a large dull-bosomed pond into which the unadorned castle-walls peep from above the trees. Such as it is, it is a place a small prince had rather keep than lose, and as I sat under the beeches—remembering that I was in the fatherland of ghost-stories—I used to fancy the warm twilight was pervaded by a thin spectral influence from this slender stream of empire, and that I could hear vague supernatural *Achs!* of regret among the bushes, and see the glimmer of broad-faced phantoms at the windows. One very hot Sunday the Emperor came, passed up the main street under several yards of red and white calico, and spent a couple of days at the Schloss. I don't know whether he saw any reproachful ghosts there, but he found, I believe, a rather scanty flesh-and-blood welcome in the town. The burgomasters measured off the proper number of festoons, and the innkeepers hung out their flags, but the townsfolk, who know their new master chiefly as the grim old wizard who has dried up the golden stream which used to flow so bounteously at the Kursaal, took an "outing" indeed, like good Germans, and stared sturdily at the show, but paid nothing for it in the way of hurrahs. The Emperor, meanwhile, rattled up and down the street in his light barouche, wearing under his white eyebrows and moustache the physiognomy of a personage quite competent to dispense with the approbation of ghosts and shopkeepers. "Homburg may have ceased to be Hessian, but evidently it is not yet Prussian," I said to a friend, and he hereupon reminded me that I was within a short distance of a more eloquent memento of the energy of Bismarck, and that I had better come over and take a look at the expiring Duchy of Darmstadt. I have followed his advice, and have been strolling about in quest of impressions. It is for the reader to say whether my impressions were worth a journey of an hour and a half.

I confess, to begin with, that they form no very terrible tale—that I saw none of the "prominent citizens" confined in chains, and no particular symptoms of the ravages of a brutal soldiery. Indeed, as you walk into the town through the grand, dull, silent street which leads from the railway station, you seem to perceive that the *genius loci* has never been frighted, like Othello's Cyprus, from its propriety. You behold it embodied in heroic bronze on the top of a huge red sandstone column, in the shape of the Grand-Duke Louis the First, who, though a very small potentate, surveys posterity from a most prodigious altitude. He was a father to his people, and some fifty years ago he "created" the *beaux quartiers* of Darmstadt, out of the midst of which his effigy rises, looking down upon the Trafalgar Square, the Place de la Concorde, of the locality. Behind him the fine, dull street pursues its course and pauses in front of the florid façade of the Schloss. This entrance into Darmstadt responds exactly to the fanciful tourist's preconceptions, and as soon as I looked up the melancholy vista, my imagination fell to rubbing its hands and to whispering that this indeed was the ghost of a little German court-city—a mouldering Modena or Ferrara of the North. I have never known a little court-city, having, by ill-luck, come into the world a day too late; but I like to think of them, to visit them in these blank, early years of their long historic sleep, and to try and guess what they must be dreaming of. They seem to murmur, as they snore everlastingly, of a very snug little social system—of gossiping whist-parties in wainscoted grand-ducal parlors, of susceptible Aulic councillors and aesthetic canonesses, of emblazoned commanders-in-chief of five hundred warriors in periwigs, of blonde young hussars, all gold-lace and billet-doux, of a miniature world of jealousies and intrigues, ceremonies and superstitions—an oppressively dull world, doubtless, to your fanciful tourist if he had been condemned to spend a month in it. But Darmstadt, obviously, was not dull to its own sense in the days before Bismarck, and doubtless the pith of its complaint of this terrible man is that he has made it so. All around Duke Louis's huge red pedestal rises a series of sober-faced palaces for the transaction of the affairs of this little empire. Before each of them is a striped red-and-white sentry-box, with a soldier in a spiked helmet mounting guard. These public offices all look highly respectable, but they have an air of sepulchral stillness. Here and there, doubtless, in their echoing chambers, is to be heard the scratching of the bureaucratic quill; but I imagine that neither the home nor the foreign affairs of Hesse-Darmstadt require nowadays an army of functionaries, and that if some grizzled old clerk were to give you an account of his avocations, they would bear a family likeness to those of Charles Lamb at the India House. There are half-a-dozen droshkies drawn up at the base of the monument, with the drivers sitting in the sun and wondering sleepily whether any one of the three persons in sight, up and down the street, will be likely to want a carriage. They wake up as I approach and look at me very hard; but they are phlegmatic German drivers, and they neither hail me with persuasive cries nor project their vehicles forcibly upon me, as would certainly be the case at Modena or Ferrara. But I pass along and ascend the street, and find something that is really, very Ferrarese. The grand-ducal Schloss rises in an immense mass out of a great crooked square, which has a very pretty likeness to an Italian *piazza*. Some of the houses have Gothic gables, and these have thrifty shop-fronts and a general air of paint and varnish; but there is shabbiness enough, and sun, and space, and bad smells, and old women under colored umbrellas selling cabbages and plums, and several persons hanging about in a professional manner, and, in the midst of it all, the great moated palace, with soldiers hanging over the parapets of the little bridges, and the inner courts used as a public thoroughfare. On one side, behind the shabby Gothic gables, is huddled that elderly Darmstadt to which Duke Louis affixed the modern mask of which his own effigy is the most eminent feature. A mask of some sort old Darmstadt most certainly needs, and it were well if it might have been one of those glass covers which in Germany are deposited over too savory dishes. The little crooked, gabled streets presume quite too audaciously on uncleanness being an element of the picturesque. The gutters stroll along with their hands in their pockets, as it were, and pause in great pools before crossings and dark archways to embrace their tributary streams, till the odorous murmur of their confluence quite smothers the voice of legend. There is dirtiness and dirtiness. Sometimes, picturesquely, it is very much to the point; but the American traveller in Germany will generally prefer not to enjoy local color in this particular form, for it unfavorably reminds him of the most sordid, the most squalid prose he knows—the corner-groceries and the region of the docks in his native metropolis.

The Schloss, however, is picturesque without abatement, and it seems to me a great pity there should not be some such monumental edifice in the middle of every town, to personify the municipal soul, as it were, to itself. If it can be beautiful, so much the better; but the Schloss at Darmstadt is ugly enough, and yet—to the eye—it amply serves its purpose. The two façades toward the square date from the middle of the last century, and are characteristically dreary and solemn, but they hide a great rambling structure of a quainter time: irregular courts, archways bearing away into darkness, a queer, great yellow bell-tower dating from the sixteenth century, a pile of multitudinous windows, roofs, and chimneys. Seen from the adjacent park, all this masses itself up into the semblance of a fantastic citadel. One rarely finds a citadel with a handsomer moat. The moat at Darmstadt yawns down out of the market-place into a deep verdurous gulf, with sloping banks of turf, on which tame shrubs are planted and mingled with the wild ones lodged in the stout foundations. It forms, indeed, below the level of the street, a charming little belt of grass and flowers. The Schloss possesses, moreover, as it properly should, a gallery of pictures, to which I proceeded to seek admission. I reflected, on my way, that it is of the first importance, picturesquely speaking, that the big building which, as I just intimated, should resume to its own sense the civic individuality of every substantial town, should always have a company of soldiers lounging under its portal and grouped about the guard-room. A green moat, a great archway, a guard-room opening out of its shadow, a couple of pacing sentinels, a group of loafing musketeers, a glimpse on one side of a sunny market-place, on the other of a dusky court—combine the objects as you may, they make a picture; they seem for the moment, as you pass, and pause, and glance, to transport you into legend. Of course the straddling men-at-arms who helped to render me this service were wearers of the spiked helmet. The Grand-Duke of Hesse-Darmstadt still occupies the Schloss, and enjoys a nominal authority. I don't know on what terms he holds it, nor what are the emotions of the grand-ducal breast when he sees a row of these peculiarly uncompromising little head-pieces bristling and twinkling under his windows. It can hardly be balm to his resentment to know that they sometimes conceal the flaxen pates of his own hereditary Hessians. The spiked helmets, of course, salute rigorously when this very limited monarch passes in and out; but I sometimes think it fortunate, under these circumstances, that the average German countenance has not a turn for ironical expression. The Duke, indeed, in susceptible moods, might take an airing in his own palace without driving abroad at all. There are apparently no end to its corridors and staircases, and I found it a long journey to the picture-gallery. I spent half an hour, to begin with, in the library, waiting till the custodian was at liberty to attend to me. The half-hour, however, was not lost, as I was entertained by a very polite librarian, with a green shade over his eyes, and as I filled my lungs, more-over, with what I was in the humor to call the atmosphere of German science. It was a very warm day, but the windows were tight-closed, in the manner of the country, and had been closed, presumably, since the days of Louis the First. The air was as dry as iron filings; it smelt of old bindings, of the insides of old books; it tasted of dust and snuff. Here and there a Herr Professor, walled in with circumjacent authorities, was burying his nose in a folio; the grey light seemed to add a coating of dust to the tiers of long, brown shelves. I came away with a headache, and that exalted esteem for the German brain, as a mere working organ, which invariably ensues upon my observation of the physical conditions of German life. I don't know that I received any very distinct impression from the picture-gallery beyond that of there being such and such a number of acres more of mouldering brush-work in the world. It was a good deal like the library, terri-bly close, and lined for room after room (it is a long series) with tiers of dusky brown canvases, on which the light of the un-washed windows seemed to turn sallow and joyless. There are a great many fine names on the frames, but they rarely correspond to anything very fine within them, though, indeed, there are several specimens of the early German school which are quite welcome (to my mind) to their assumed "originality." Early or late, German art rarely seems to me a happy adventure. Two or three of the rooms were filled with large examples of the modern German landscape school, before which I lingered, but not for the pleasure of it. I was reflecting that the burden of French philosophy just now is the dogma that the Germans are a race of *faux bonshommes*; that their transcendental aesthetics are a mere kicking up of dust to cover their picking and stealing; and that their frank-souled naïveté is no better than a sharper's "alias." I don't pretend to weigh the charge in a general sense, but I certainly think that a good French patriot, in my place, would have cried out that he had caught the hypocrites in the act. These blooming views of Switzerland and Italy seemed to me the most dishonest things in the world, and I was puzzled to understand how so very innocent an affair as a landscape in oils could be made such a vehicle of offence. These were extremely clever; the art of shuffling away trouble has rarely been brought to greater perfection. It is evidently an elaborate system; there is a school; the pictures were all from different hands, and the precious receipt had been passed round the circle.

But why should I talk of bad pictures since I brought away from Darmstadt the memory of one of the best in the world? It forms the sole art-treasure of the place, and I duly went in quest of it; but I kept it in reserve as one keeps the best things, and meanwhile I strolled in the Herrengarten. The fondness of Germans for a garden, wherever a garden can be conceived, is one of their most amiable characteristics, and I should be curious to know how large a section of the total soil of the fatherland is laid out in rusty lawns and gravel-paths, and adorned with beechen groves and bowers. The garden-hours of one's life, as I may say, are not the least agreeable, and there are more garden-hours in German lives than in most others. But I shall not describe my garden-hours at Darmstadt. Part of them was spent in walking around the theatre, which stands close beside the Schloss, with its face upon the square and its back among the lawns and bowers. The theatre, in the little court-city of my regrets, is quite an affair of state, and the manager second only in importance to the prime-minister or the commander-in-chief. Or rather the Grand Duke is manager himself, and the leading actress, as a matter of course, his morganatic wife. The present Grand-Duke of Hesse-Darmstadt, I believe, is a zealous patron of the drama, and maintains a troupe of comedians, who doubtless do much to temper the dulness of his capital. The present theatre is simply a picturesque ruin, having been lately burned down, for all the world like an American "opera-house." But the actors have found a provisional refuge, and I have just been presented with the programme of the opening night of the winter season. I saw the rest of Darmstadt as I took my way to the palace of Prince Karl. It was a very quiet pilgrimage, and I perhaps met three people in the long, dull, proper street through which it led me. One of them was a sentinel with a spiked helmet marching before the snug little palace of the Prince Louis—the gentleman who lately married the Princess Alice of England. Another was a school-boy in spectacles, nursing a green bag full of polyglot exercises, I suppose, of whom I asked my way; and the third was the sturdy little musketeer who was trying to impart a *reflet* of authority to the neat little white house occupied by the Prince Earl. But this frowning soldier is no proper symbol of the kindly custom of the house. I was admitted unconditionally, ushered into the little drawing-room, and allowed half an hour's undisturbed contemplation of the beautiful Holbein— the famous picture of the Meyer family. The reader interested in such matters may remember the discussion maintained two years since, at the time of the general exhibition of the younger Holbein's works in Dresden, as to the respective merits—and I believe the presumptive priority in date—of this Darmstadt picture and the presentation of the same theme which adorns the Dresden Gallery. I forget how the question was settled— whether, indeed, it was settled at all, and I have never seen the Dresden picture; but it seems to me that if I were to choose a Holbein, this one would content me. It represents a sort of plainly lovely Virgin holding her child, crowned with a kind of gorgeous episcopal crown, and worshipped by six kneeling figures—the worthy Goodman Meyer, his wife, and their progenitors. It is a wonderfully solid masterpiece, and so full of wholesome human substance that I should think its owner could go about his daily work the better—eat and drink and sleep and perform the various functions of life more largely and smoothly—for having it constantly before his eyes. I was not disappointed, and I may now confess that my errand at Darmstadt had been much more to see the *Holbeinische Gemälde* than to examine the trail of the serpent—the footprints of Bismarck.

AUTUMN IN FLORENCE

November 15, 1874

Florence from the Arno.

FLORENCE, TOO, HAS ITS "SEASON" AS WELL AS ROME, AND I have been taking some satisfaction, for the past six weeks, in the thought that it has not yet begun. Coming here in the first days of October, I found the summer lingering on in almost untempered force, and ever since, until within a day or two, it has been dying a very gradual death. Properly enough, as the city of flowers, Florence is delightful in the spring—during those blossoming weeks of March and April, when a six months' steady shivering has not shaken New York and Boston free of the grip of

winter. But something in the mood of autumn seems to suit peculiarly the mood in which an appreciative tourist strolls through
these many-memoried streets and galleries and churches. Old
things, old places, old people (or, at least, old races) have always
seemed to me to tell their secrets more freely in such moist, gray,
melancholy days as have formed the complexion of the past October. With Christmas comes the winter, the opera (the good
opera), the gaieties, American and other. Meanwhile, it is pleasant enough, for persons fond of the Florentine flavor, that the
opera is indifferent, that the Americans have not all arrived, and
that the weather has a monotonous, overcast softness, extremely
favorable to contemplative habits. There is no crush on the Cas-
cine, as on the sunny days of winter, and the Arno, wandering
away toward the mountains in the haze, seems as shy of being
looked at as a good picture in a bad light. No light could be better to my eyes; it seems the faded light of that varied past on
which an observer here spends so many glances. There are
people, I know, who freely intimate that the "Florentine flavor" I
speak of is dead and buried, and that it is an immense misfortune
not to have tasted the real thing, in the Grand Duke's time.
Some of these friends of mine have been living here ever since,
and have seen the little historic city expanding in the hands of
its "enterprising" syndic into its shining girdle of boulevards and
beaux quartiers, such as M. Haussmann set the fashion of—like
some precious little page of antique text swallowed up in a mar-

ginal commentary. I am not sure of the real wisdom of regretting the change—apart from its being always good sense to prefer a larger city to a smaller one. For Florence, in its palmy days, was peculiarly a city of change—of shifting régimes, and policies, and humors; and the Florentine character, as we have it to-day, is a character which takes all things easily for having seen so many come and go. It saw the national capital arrive, and took no further thought than sufficed for the day; it saw it depart, and whistled it cheerfully on its way to Rome. The new boulevards of the Sindaco Peruzzi come, it may be said, but they don't go; but after all, from the aesthetic point of view, it is not strictly necessary they should. It seems to me part of the essential amiability of Florence—of her genius for making you take to your favor on easy terms everything that in any way belongs to her—that she has already flung a sort of *reflet* of her charm over all their undried mortar and plaster.

Nothing could be prettier, in a modern way, than the Piazza d'Azeglio, or the Avenue of the Princess Margaret; nothing pleasanter than to stroll across them, and enjoy the afternoon lights through their liberal vistas. They carry you close to the charming hills which look down into Florence on all sides, and if, in the foreground, your sense is a trifle perplexed by the white pavements, dotted here and there with a policeman or a nurse-maid, you have only to look just beyond to see Fiesole on its mountainside glowing purple from the opposite sunset.

Turning back into Florence proper, you have local color enough and to spare—which you enjoy the more, doubtless, from standing off in this fashion to get your light and your point of view. The elder streets, abutting on all this newness, go boring away into the heart of the city in narrow, dusky vistas of a fascinating picturesqueness. Pausing to look down them, sometimes, and to penetrate the deepening shadows through which they recede, they seem to me little corridors leading out from the past, as mystical as the ladder in Jacob's dream; and when I see a single figure coming up toward me I am half afraid to wait till it arrives; it seems too much like a ghost—a messenger from an under-world. Florence, paved with its great mosaics of slabs, and lined with its massive Tuscan palaces, which, in their large dependence on pure symmetry for beauty of effect, reproduce more than other modern styles the simple nobleness of Greek architecture, must have always been a stately city, and not especially rich in that ragged picturesqueness—the picturesqueness of poverty—on which we feast our idle eyes at Rome and Naples. Except in the unfinished fronts of the churches, which, however, unfortunately, are mere prosaic ugliness, one finds here less romantic stateliness than in most Italian cities. But at two or three points it exists in perfection—in just such perfection as proves that often what is literally hideous may be constructively delightful. On the north side of the Arno, between the Ponte Vecchio and the Ponte Santa Trinità, is an ancient row of houses, backing on the river, in whose yellow flood they bathe their aching old feet. Anything more battered and be-fouled, more cracked and disjointed, dirtier, drearier, shabbier, it would be impossible to conceive. They look as if, fifty years ago, the muddy river had risen over their chimneys, and then subsided again and left them coated for ever with its unsightly slime. And yet, forsooth, because the river is yellow, and the light is yellow, and here and there, elsewhere, some mellow, mouldering surface, some hint of color, some accident of atmo-sphere, takes up the foolish tale and repeats the note—because, in short, it is Florence, it is Italy, and you are an American, bred amid the micaceous sparkle of brownstone fronts and lavish of enthusiasms, these miserable dwellings, instead of simply sug-gesting mental invocations to an enterprising board of health, bloom and glow all along the line in the perfect felicity of pic-turesqueness. Lately, during the misty autumn nights, the moon has been shining on them faintly, and refining away their shab-biness into something ineffably strange and spectral. The yellow river sweeps along without a sound, and the pale tenements hang above it like a vague miasmatic exhalation. The dimmest back-scene at the opera, when the tenor is singing his sweetest, seems hardly to belong to a more dreamily fictitious world.

What it is that infuses so rich an interest into the charm of Florence is difficult to say in a few words; yet as one wanders hither and thither in quest of a picture or a bas-relief, it seems no marvel that the place should be interesting. Two industrious English ladies have lately published a couple of volumes of "Walks" through the Florentine streets, and their work is a long enumeration of great artistic deeds. These things remain for the most part in sound preservation, and, as the weeks go by and you spend a constant portion of your days among them, you seem really to be living in the magical time. It was not long; it lasted, in its splendor, for less than a century; but it has stored away in the palaces and churches of Florence a heritage of beauty which these three enjoying centuries since have not yet come to the end of. This forms a distinct intellectual atmosphere, into which you may turn aside from the modern world and fill your lungs with the breath of a forgotten creed. The memorials of the past in Florence have the advantage of being somehow more cheerful and exhilarating than in other cities which have had a great aesthetic period. Venice, with her old palaces cracking with the weight of their treasures, is, in its influence, insupportably sad; Athens, with her maimed marbles and dishonored memories, transmutes the consciousness of sensitive observers, I am told, into a chronic heartache. But in one's impression of old Florence there is something very sound and sweet and wholesome—something which would make it a growing pleasure to live here long. In Athens and Venice, surely, a long residence would be a pain. The reason of this is partly the peculiarly lovable, gentle character of Florentine art in general—partly the tenderness of time, in its lapse, which, save in a few cases, has been as sparing of injury as if it knew that when it had dimmed and corroded these charming things, it would have nothing so sweet again for its tooth to feed on. If the beautiful Ghirlandaios and Lippis are fading, we shall never know it. The large Fra Angelico in the Academy is as clear and keen as if the good old monk were standing there wiping his brushes; the colors seem to *sing*, as it were, like new-fledged birds in June. Nothing is more character-istic of early Tuscan art than the bas-reliefs of Luca della Rob-bia; yet, save for their innocence, there is not one of them that might not have been modelled yesterday. The color is mild but not faded, the forms are simple but not archaic. But perhaps the best image of the absence of stale melancholy in Florentine an-tiquity is the bell-tower of Giotto beside the Cathedral. No trav-eller has forgotten how it stands there, straight and slender, plated with colored marbles, seemingly so strangely rich, in the common streets. It is not even simple in design, and I never cease to wonder that the painter of so many grimly archaic little frescoes should have fashioned a building which, in the way of elaborate elegance, leaves the finest modern culture nothing to suggest. Nothing can be imagined at once more lightly and more richly fanciful; it might have been a present, ready-made, to the city by some Oriental genie. Yet, with its Eastern look, it seems of no particular time; it is not gray and hoary like a Gothic spire, nor cracked and despoiled like a Greek temple; its marbles shine so little less freshly than when they were laid together, and the sunset lights up its embroidered cornice with such a friendly radiance, that you come to regard it at last as simply the graceful, indestructible soul of the city made visible. The Cathedral, externally, in spite of its solemn hugeness, strikes the same light, cheerful note; it has grandeur, of course, but such a pleasant, agreeable, ingenuous grandeur. It has seen so much, and outlived so much, and served so many sad purposes, and yet remains in aspect so true to the gentle epicureanism that conceived it. Its vast, many-colored marble walls are one of the sweetest entertainments of Florence; there is an endless fascination in walking past them, and feeling them lift their great acres of mosaic higher in the air than you care to look. You greet them as you do the side of a mountain when you are walking in the valley; you don't twist back your head to look at the top, but content yourself with some little nestling hollow—some especial combination of the little marble dominoes.

Florence is richer in pictures than one really knows until one has begun to look for them in outlying corners. Then, here and there, one comes upon treasures which it almost seems as if one might pilfer for the New York Museum without their being missed. The Pitti Palace, of course, is a collection of masterpieces; they jostle each other in their splendor, and they rather weary your admiration. The Uffizi is almost as fine a show, and together with that long serpentine artery which crosses the Arno and connects them, they form the great central treasure-chamber of the city. But I have been neglecting them of late for the sake of the Academy, where there are fewer copyists and tourists, fewer of the brilliant things you don't care for. I observed here, a day or two since, lurking obscurely in one of the smaller rooms, a most enchanting Sandro Botticelli. It had a mean black frame, and it was hung where no one would have looked for a master-piece; but a good glass brought out its merits. It represented the walk of Tobias with the Angel, and there are parts of it really that an angel might have painted. Placed as it is, I doubt whether it is noticed by half-a-dozen persons a year. What a pity that it should not become the property of an institution which would give it a brave gilded frame and a strong American light! Then it might shed its wonderful beauty with all the force of rare ex-ample. Botticelli is, in a certain way, the most interesting of the Florentine painters—the only one, save Leonardo and Michael Angelo, who had a really inventive fancy. His imagination has a complex turn, which gives him at first a strangely modern, famil-iar air, but we soon discover that what we know of him is what our contemporary Pre-Raphaelites have borrowed. When we read Mr. William Morris's poetry, when we look at Mr. Rossetti's pictures, we are enjoying, among other things, a certain amount of diluted Botticelli. He endeavored much more than the other early Florentines to make his faces express a mood, a conscious-ness, and it is the beautiful preoccupied type of face which we find in his pictures that our modern Pre-Raphaelites reproduce, with their own modifications. Fra Angelico, Filippo Lippi, Ghirlandaio, were not imaginative; but who was ever more devotedly observant, more richly, genially graphic? If there should ever be a great weeding out of the world's possessions, I should pray that the best works of the early Florentine school be counted among the flowers. With the ripest performances of the Venetians, they seem to me the most valuable things in the history of art. Heaven forbid that we should be narrowed down to a cruel choice; but if it came to a question of keeping or losing between half-a-dozen Raphaels and half-a-dozen things I could select at the Academy, I am afraid that, for myself, the memory of the "Transfiguration" would not save the Raphaels. And yet this was not the opinion of a patient artist whom I saw the other day copying the finest of Ghirlandaios—a beautiful "Adoration of the Kings" at the Hospital of the Innocenti. This is another specimen of the buried art-wealth of Florence. It hangs in a dusky chapel, far aloft, behind an altar, and, though now and then a stray tourist wanders in and puzzles awhile over the vaguely glowing forms, the picture is never really seen and enjoyed. I found an aged Frenchman of modest mien perched on the little platform beneath it, behind a great hedge of altar candlesticks, with an admirable copy almost completed. The difficulties of his task had been almost insuperable, and his performance seemed to me a real feat of magic. He could scarcely see or move, and he could only find room for his canvas by rolling it together and painting a small piece at a time, so that he never enjoyed a view of his work as a whole. The original is gorgeous with color and bewildering with ornamental detail, but not a gleam of the painter's crimson was wanting, not a curl in his gold arabesque. It seemed to me that, if I had copied a Ghirlandaio under such circumstances, I should at least maintain, for my credit, that he was the first painter in the world. "Very good of its kind," said the weary old man, with a shrug, in reply to my raptures; "but oh! how far short of Raphael!" However that may be, if the reader ever observes this brilliant copy in the Museum of Copies in Paris, let him stop before it with a certain reverence; it is one of the patient things of art. Seeing it wrought there, in its dusky chapel, in such scanty convenience, seemed to remind me that the old art-life of Florence was not yet extinct. The old painters are dead, but their influence is living.

TUSCAN CITIES
April 18, 1874

Cathedral Square, Pisa, Italy.

T HE CITIES I MEAN ARE LEGHORN, PISA, LUCCA, AND PISTOIA, among which I have been spending the last few days. The most striking fact as to Leghorn, it must be conceded at the out-set, is that, being in Tuscany, it should be so scantily Tuscan. The traveller curious in local color must content himself with the deep blue expanse of the Mediterranean. The streets, away from the docks, are modern, genteel, and rectangular. Liverpool might acknowledge them if it were not for their fresh-colored stucco. They are the offspring of the new industry, which is death to the old idleness. Of picturesque architecture, fruit of the old idleness, or at least of the old leisure, Leghorn is singularly destitute. It has neither a church worth one's attention, nor a municipal palace, nor a museum, and it may claim the distinction, unique in Italy, of being the city of no pictures. In a shabby corner, near the docks, stands a statue of one of the elder grand-dukes of Tuscany, appealing to posterity on grounds now vague—chiefly that of having placed certain Moors under tribute. Four colossal negroes, in very bad bronze, are chained to the base of the monument, which forms with their assistance a sufficiently fantastic group; but to patronize the arts is not the line of the Livornese, and, for want of the slender annuity which would keep its precinct sacred, this curious memorial is buried in docks and rubbish. I must add that, on the other hand, there is a very well-conditioned and, in attitude and gesture, extremely realistic statue of Cavour in one of the city squares, and a couple of togaed effigies of recent grand-dukes in another. Leghorn is a city of magnificent spaces, and it was so long a journey from the sidewalk to the pedestal of these images that I never took the time to go and read the inscriptions. And in truth, vaguely, I bore the originals a grudge, and wished to know as little about them as possible; for it seemed to me that as *patres patriae*, in their degree, they might have decreed that the great blank, ochre-faced *piazza* should be a trifle less ugly. There is a distinct amenity, however, in any experience of Italy, and I shall probably in the future not be above sparing a light regret to several of the hours of which the one I speak of was composed. I shall remember a large, cool, bourgeois villa in a garden, in a noiseless suburb—a middle-aged villa, roomy and stony, as an Italian villa should be. I shall remember that, as I sat in the garden, and, looking up from my book, saw through a gap in the shrubbery the red house-tiles against the deep blue sky and the gray underside of the ilex leaves turned up by the Mediterranean breeze, I had a vague consciousness that I was not in the Western world.

If you should happen to wish to do so, you must not go to Pisa, and indeed we are most of us forewarned as to Pisa from an early age. Few of us can have had a childhood so unblessed by contact with the arts as that one of its occasional diversions should not have been a puzzled scrutiny of some alabaster model of the Leaning Tower under a glass cover in a back-parlor. Pisa and its monuments have, in other words, been industriously vulgarized, but it is astonishing how well they have survived the process. The charm of Pisa is, in fact, a charm of a high order, and is but partially foreshadowed by the famous crookedness of its *campanile*. I felt it irresistibly and yet almost inexpressibly the other afternoon, as I made my way to the classic corner of the city through the warm, drowsy air which nervous people come to inhale as a sedative. I was with an invalid companion, who had had no sleep to speak of for a fortnight. "Ah! stop the carriage," said my friend, gaping, as I could feel, deliciously, "in the shadow of this old slumbering palazzo, and let me sit here and close my eyes, and taste for an hour of oblivion." Once strolling over the grass, however, out of which the four marble monuments rise, we awaked responsively enough to the present hour. Most people remember the happy remark of tasteful, old-fashioned Forsyth (who touched a hundred other points in his "Italy" hardly less happily) as to three beautiful buildings being "fortunate alike in their society and their solitude." It must be admitted that they are more fortunate in their society than we felt ourselves to be in ours, for the scene presented the animated appearance for which, on any fine spring day, all the choicest haunts of ancient quietude in Italy are becoming yearly more remarkable. There were clamorous beggars at all the sculptured portals and bait for beggars, in abundance, trailing in and out of them under convoy of loquacious *ciceroni*. I forget just how I apportioned the responsibility of intrusion, for it was not long before fellow-tourists and fellow-countrymen became a vague, deadened, muffled presence, like the dentist's last words when he is giving you ether. They suffered a sort of mystical disintegration in the dense, bright, tranquil atmosphere of the place. The cathedral and its companions are fortunate indeed in everything—fortunate in the spacious angle of the gray old city-wall, which folds about them in their sculptured elegance like a strong protecting arm; fortunate in the broad green sward which stretches from the marble base of cathedral and cemetery to the rugged foot of the rampart; fortunate in the little vagabonds who dot the grass, plucking daisies and exchanging Italian cries; fortunate in the pale-gold tone to which time and the soft sea-damp have mellowed and darkened their marble plates; fortunate, above all, in an indescribable gracefulness of grouping (half-hazard, half-design), which ensures them, in one's memory of things admired, very much the same isolated corner which they occupy in the pleasant city.

Of the smaller cathedrals of Italy, I know none that I prefer to that of Pisa; none which, on a moderate scale, produces more the impression of a great church. Indeed, it seems externally of such moderate size that one is surprised at its grandeur of effect within. An architect of genius, for all that he works with colossal blocks and cumbrous pillars, is certainly the most cunning of all artists. The façade of the cathedral of Pisa is a small pyramidal screen, covered with delicate carvings and chasings, distributed over a series of short columns upholding narrow arches. It looks like an imitation of goldsmith's work in stone, and the space covered is apparently so small that there seems a fitness in the dainty labor. How it is that on the inner side of this façade the wall should appear to rise to a splendid height, and to support one end of a ceiling as remote in its gilded grandeur, one could almost fancy, as that of St. Peter's; how it is that the nave should stretch away in such solemn vastness, the shallow transepts carry out the grand impression, and the apse of the choir hollow itself out like a dusky cavern fretted with golden stalactites—all this must be expounded by a keener architectural analyst than I. To sit somewhere against a pillar, where the vista is large and the incidents cluster richly, and vaguely resolve these mysteries without answering them, is the best of one's usual enjoyment of a great church. It takes no great ingenuity to conjecture that a gigantic Byzantine Christ, in mosaic, on the concave roof of the choir, contributes largely to the impressiveness of the place. It has even more of stiff solemnity than is common to works of its school, and it made me wonder more than ever what the human mind could have been when such unlovely forms could satisfy its conception of holiness. There seems something truly pathetic in the fate of these huge mosaic idols, and in the change that has befallen our manner of acceptance of them. It is a singular contrast between the original sublimity of their pretensions and the way in which they flatter that audacious sense of the grotesque which the modern imagination has smuggled even into the appreciation of religious forms. They were meant to be hardly less grand than the Deity itself, but the only part they play now is to mark the further end of our progress in spiritual refinement. The two limits, on this line, are admirably represented in the choir at Pisa, by the flat gilded Christ on the roof and the beautiful specimen of the painter Sodoma on the wall. The latter, a small picture of the Sacrifice of Isaac, is one of the best examples of its exquisite author, and perhaps, as chance has it, the most perfect opposition that could be found to the spirit of the great mosaic. There are many painters more power-ful than Sodoma—painters who, like the author of the mosaic, attempted and compassed grandeur; but none possess a more persuasive grace, none more than he have sifted and chastened their conception till it exhales the sweetness of a perfectly dis-tilled perfume.

Of the patient successive efforts of painting to arrive at the supreme refinement of Sodoma, the Campo Santo hard by offers a most interesting memorial. It presents a long, blank marble wall to the relative profaneness of the cathedral close, but within it is a perfect treasure-house of art. A long quadrangle surrounds an open court, where weeds and wild-roses are tan-gled together, and a sunny stillness seems to rest consentingly, as if nature had been won to consciousness of the precious relics committed to her. Something in the place reminded me of the collegiate cloisters of Oxford; but it must be confessed that this is a handsome compliment to Oxford. The open arches of the quadrangles of Magdalen and Christ Church are not of mellow Carrara marble, nor do their columns, slim and elegant, seem to frame the unglazed windows of a cathedral. To be buried in the Campo Santo of Pisa you need only be illustrious, and there is liberal allowance both as to the character and degree of your fame. The most obtrusive object in one of the long vistas is a most complicated monument to Madame Catalani, the singer, recently erected by her (possibly) too appreciative heirs. The wide pavement is a mosaic of sepulchral slabs, and the walls, below the base of the paling frescoes, are encrusted with inscriptions and encumbered with urns and antique sarcophagi. The place is at once a cemetery and a museum, and its especial charm is its strange mixture of the active and the passive, of art and rest, of life and death. Originally its walls were one vast continuity of closely-pressed frescoes, but now the great capricious scars and stains have come to outnumber the pictures, and the cemetery has grown to be a burial-place of pulverized masterpieces as well as of finished lives. The fragments of painting that remain are, however, fortunately the best; for one is safe in believing that a host of undimmed neighbors would distract but little from the two great works of Orcagna. Most people know the "Triumph of Death" and the "Last Judgment" from descriptions and engravings; but to measure the possible good faith of imitative art, one must stand there and see the painter's howling potentates dragged into hell in all the vividness of his bright, hard coloring; see his feudal courtiers on their palfreys, holding their noses at what they are so fast coming to; see his great Christ, in judgment, deny forgiveness with a gesture commanding enough to extinguish the idea. The charge that Michael Angelo borrowed his cursing Saviour from this great figure of Orcagna is more valid than most accusations of plagiarism; but of the two figures one at least could be spared. For direct, triumphant expressiveness these two superb frescoes have probably never been surpassed. The painter aims at no very delicate meanings, but he drives certain gross ones home so effectively that for a parallel to his skill one must look to the stage.

On the other side of the cloister one finds the beautiful frescoes of Benozzo Gozzoli. If Orcagna's work was elected to survive the ravages of time, it is a happy chance that it should be balanced by a group of performances of such a different temper. The contrast is the more striking that, in subject, the work of both painters is narrowly theological. But Benozzo cares in his theology for nothing but the story, the scene, and the drama— the chance to pile up palaces and spires in his backgrounds against pale-blue skies cross-barred with pearly, fleecy clouds, and to scatter sculptured arches and shady trellises over the front, with every incident of human life going forward lightly and gracefully beneath them. Lightness and grace are the painter's great qualities; and, if we had to characterize him briefly, we might say that he marks the hithermost limit of unconscious elegance. His charm is natural fineness; a little more, and we should have refinement—which is a very different thing. Like all *les délicats* of this world, as M. Renan calls them, Bonozzo has suffered greatly. The space on the walls he originally covered with his Old Testament stories is immense; but his exquisite handiwork has peeled off by the acre, as one may almost say, and the latter compartments of the series are swallowed up in huge white scars, out of which a helpless head or hand peeps forth, like those of creatures sinking into a quicksand. As for Pisa at large, although it is not exactly what one would call a mouldering city—for it has a certain well-aired cleanness and brightness, even in its supreme tranquillity—it affects the imagination in very much the same way as the Campo Santo. And, in truth, a city so ancient and deeply historic as Pisa is at every step but the burial-ground of a larger life than its present one. The wide, empty streets, the gaudy Tuscan palaces (which look as if about all of them there were a genteel private understanding, independent of placards, that they are to be let extremely cheap), the delicious relaxing air, the full-flowing yellow river, the lounging Pisani smelling, metaphorically, their poppy-flowers, seemed to me all so many admonitions to resignation and oblivion. And this is what I mean by saying that the charm of Pisa (apart from its cluster of monuments) is a charm of a high order. The architecture is not especially curious; the lions are few; there are no fixed points for stopping and gaping. And yet the impression is profound; the charm is a moral charm. If I were ever to be incurably disappointed in life; if I had lost my health, my money, or my friends; if I were resigned, for evermore, to pitching my expectations in a minor key, I think I should go and live at Pisa. Something in the atmosphere would assent most soothingly to my mind. Its quietude would seem something more than a stillness—a hush. Pisa may be a dull place to live in, but it is a capital place to wait for death.

Nothing could be more charming than the country between Pisa and Lucca—unless possibly it is the country between Lucca and Pistoia. If Pisa is dead Tuscany, Lucca is Tuscany still living and enjoying, desiring and intending. The town is a charming mixture of antique picturesqueness and modern animation; and not only the town, but the country—the blooming, romantic country which you behold from the famous promenade on the city-wall. The wall is of superbly solid brickwork and of extraordinary breadth, and its summit, planted with goodly trees, and swelling here and there into bastions and little open gardens, surrounds the city with a circular lounging-place of extreme picturesqueness. This well-kept, shady, ivy-grown rampart reminded me of certain mossy corners of England; but it looks away to a prospect of more than English loveliness—a broad, green plain, where the summer yields a double crop of grain, and a circle of bright blue mountains speckled with high-hung convents and profiled castles and nestling villas, and traversed by valleys of a deeper and duskier blue. In one of the deepest and shadiest of these valleys a charming watering-place is hidden away yet awhile longer from railways, the baths to which Lucca has given its name. Lucca is pre-eminently a city of churches, ecclesiastical architecture being, indeed, the only one of the arts to which it seems to have given attention. There are picturesque bits of domestic architecture, but no great palaces, and no importunate frequency of pictures. The cathedral, however, is a résumé of the merits of its companions, and is a singularly noble and interesting church. Its peculiar boast is a wonderful inlaid front, on which horses and hounds and hunted beasts are lavishly figured in black marble over a white ground. What I chiefly enjoyed in the gray solemnity of the nave and transepts was the superb effect of certain second-story Gothic arches (those which rest on the pavement are Lombard). These arches are delicate and slender, like those of the cloister at Pisa, and they play their part in the dusky upper air with real sublimity.

At Pistoia there is, of course, a cathedral, and there is nothing unexpected in its being, externally at least, a very picturesque one; in its having a grand campanile at its door, a gaudy baptistery, in alternate layers of black and white marble, across the way, and a stately civic palace on either side. But even if I had the space to do otherwise, I should prefer to speak less of the particular objects of interest at Pistoia than of the pleasure I found it to lounge away in the empty streets the quiet hours of a warm afternoon. To say where I lingered longest would be to tell of a little square before the hospital, out of which you look up at the beautiful frieze in colored earthenware by the brothers

Della Robbia, which runs across the front of the building. It represents the seven orthodox offices of charity, and with its brilliant blues and yellows, and its tender expressiveness, it brightens up amazingly the sense and soul of this little gray corner of the mediaeval city. Pistoia is still strictly mediaeval. How grass-grown it seemed, how drowsy, how full of idle Sisters and melancholy monks! If nothing was supremely wonderful, everything was delicious.

RAVENNA
June 8, 1874

The Mausoleum of Galla Placidia in Ravenna, ca. 1910.

I WRITE THESE LINES ON A COLD SWISS MOUNTAIN-TOP, SHUT in by an intense white mist from any glimpse of the under-world of lovely Italy; but as I jotted down the other day, in the ancient capital of Honorius and Theodoric, the few notes of which they are composed, I let the original date stand for local color's sake. Its mere look, as I transcribe it, emits a grateful glow in the midst of the Alpine rawness, and gives a depressed imagination something tangible to grasp while awaiting the return of fine weather. For Ravenna was glowing, less than a week since, as I edged along the narrow strip of shadow binding one side of the empty, white streets. After a long, chilly spring, the summer this year descended upon Italy with a sudden jump and a terrible vehemence of purpose. I stole away from Florence in the night, and even on top of the Apennines, under the dull starlight and in the rushing train, one could but sit and pant perspiringly. At Bologna I found a festa, or rather two festas, a civil and a religious, going on in mutual mistrust and disparagement. The civil one was the now legal Italian holiday of the Statuto; the religious, a jubilee of certain local churches. The latter is observed by the Bolognese parishes in couples, and comes round for each couple but once in ten years—an arrangement by which the faithful at large ensure themselves a liberal recurrence of expensive processions. It was not my business to distinguish the sheep from the goats, the prayers from the scoffers; it was enough that, melting together under the scorching sun, they made the picturesque city doubly picturesque. The combination at one point was really dramatic. While a long procession of priests and young virgins in white veils bearing tapers was being organized in one of the streets, a review of the King's troops was going on outside of the town. On its return, a large detachment of cavalry passed across the space where the incense was burning, the pictured banners swaying, and the litany being droned, and checked the advance of the little ecclesiastical troop. The long vista of the street, between the porticoes, was festooned with garlands and scarlet and tinsel; the robes and crosses and canopies of the priests, the clouds of perfumed smoke, and the white veils of the maidens, were resolved by the hot, bright air into a gorgeous medley of colors, across which the mounted soldiers went rattling and flashing like a conquering army trampling over an embassy of propitiation. It was, to tell the truth, the first time an Italian festa had worn to my eyes that warmth of coloring, that pictorial confusion, which tradition promises; and I confess that my eyes found more pleasure in it than they found an hour later in those masterpieces of the Bolognese school which hang in the Pinacotheca.

For Ravenna, however, I had nothing but smiles—grave, philosophic smiles, such as accord with the tranquil, melancholy interest of the place. I arrived there in the evening, before, even at drowsy Ravenna, the festa of the Statuto had altogether put itself to bed. I immediately strolled forth from the inn, and found it sitting up a while longer on the piazza, chiefly at the café door, listening to the band of the garrison by the light of a dozen or so of feeble tapers, fastened along the front of the palace of the Government. Before long, however, it had dispersed and departed, and I was left alone with the grey illumination and with an affable citizen, whose testimony as to the manners and customs of Ravenna I had aspired to obtain. I had already observed to sufficient purpose to borrow confidence to suggest deferentially that it was not the liveliest place in the world, and my friend admitted that in fact it was a trifle sluggish. But had I seen the Corso? Without seeing the Corso it was unfair to conclude against Ravenna. The Corso of Ravenna, of a hot summer night, had an air of surprising seclusion and repose. Here and there in an upper, closed window glimmered a light; my companion's footsteps and my own were the only sounds; not a creature was within sight. The suffocating atmosphere helped me to believe for a moment that I was walking in the Italy of Boccaccio, hand-in-hand with the plague, through a city which had lost half its population by pestilence and the other half by flight. I turned back into my inn, profoundly satisfied. This at last was old-world dulness of a prime distillation; this at last was antiquity, history, repose.

This impression was largely confirmed and enriched on the following day; but it was obliged, at an early stage of my explorations, to give precedence to another—the lively realization, namely, of my imperfect acquaintance with Gibbon and other cognate authorities. At Ravenna, the waiter at the café and the coachman who drives you to the Pine-Forest allude to Galla Placidia and Justinian as to any attractive topic of the hour; wherever you turn you encounter some peremptory challenge to your accomplishments in chronology. For myself, I could only attune my intellect vaguely to the intensely historical character of the place—I could only feel that I was breathing an atmosphere of records and relics. I conned my guide-book and looked up at the great mosaics, and then fumbled at poor Murray again for some intenser light on the court of Justinian; but I can imagine that to a visitor more intimate with the originals of the various great almond-eyed mosaic portraits in the vaults of the churches, these extremely curious works of art may have a really formidable interest. I found Ravenna looking by daylight like a vast, straggling, depopulated village. The streets with hardly an exception are grass-grown, and though I walked about all day I failed to perceive a single wheeled vehicle. I remember no shop but the little establishment of an urbane photographer, whose views of the Pine-Forest gave me an irresistible desire to transport myself thither. There is no architecture to speak of, and though there are a great many large domiciles with aristocratic names, they stand cracking and baking in the sun in no very comfortable fashion. The houses for the most part have a half-rustic look; they are low and meagre and shabby and interspersed with high garden walls, over which the long arms of tangled vines hang motionless into the stagnant streets. Here and there in all this dreariness, in some particularly silent and grassy corner, rises an old brick church with a façade more or less spoiled by cheap modernization, and a strange cylindrical campanile, pierced with small arched windows and extremely suggestive of the fifth century. These churches constitute the palpable interest of Ravenna, and their own principal interest, after thirteen centuries of well-intentioned spoliation, resides in their unequalled collection of early Christian mosaics. It is in a certain sense a curiously simple interest, and it leads one's reflections along a narrow and definite channel. There are older churches in Rome, and churches which, looked at as museums, are more variously and richly entertaining; but in Rome you stumble at every step upon some curious pagan memorial, often beautiful enough to lead your thoughts wandering far from the primitive rigidities of the Christian faith.

Ravenna, on the other hand, began with the church, and all its monuments and relics are harmoniously rigid. By the middle of the first century it possessed an exemplary saint—Apollinaris, a disciple of Peter—to whom its two finest churches are dedicated. It was to one of these, jocosely entitled the "new" one, that I first directed my steps. I lingered outside a while and looked at the great red, barrel-shaped bell-towers, so rusty, so crumbling, so archaic, and yet so resolute to ring in another century or two, and then went in to the coolness, the shining marble columns, the queer old sculptured slabs and sarcophagi, and the long mosaics, scintillating under the roof, along the wall of the nave. San Apollinare Nuovo, like most of its companions, is a magazine of early Christian odds and ends; of fragments of yellow marble encrusted with quaint sculptured emblems of primitive dogma; great rough troughs, containing the bones of old bishops; episcopal chairs with the marble worn narrow with centuries of pressure from the solid episcopal person; slabs from the fronts of old pulpits, covered with carven hieroglyphics of an almost Egyptian abstruseness—lambs, and stags, and fishes, and beasts of theological affinities even less apparent. Upon all these strange things the strange figures in the great mosaic panorama look down, with colored cheeks and staring eyes, lifelike enough to speak to you and answer your wonderment, and tell you in bad Latin of the decadence that it was in such and such a fashion they believed and worshipped. First, on each side, near the door, are houses and ships and various old landmarks of Ravenna; then begins a long procession, on one side, of twenty-two white-robed virgins and three obsequious magi, terminating in a throne bearing the Madonna and Child, surrounded by four angels; on the other side, of an equal number of male saints (twenty-five, that is) holding crowns in their hands and leading to the Saviour, enthroned between angels of singular expressiveness. What it is these long, slim seraphs express I cannot quite say, but they have an odd, knowing, sidelong look out of the narrow ovals of their eyes which, though not without sweetness, would certainly make me feel like murmuring a defensive prayer or so if I were to find myself alone in the church toward dusk. All this work is of the latter part of the sixth century and brilliantly preserved. The gold backgrounds twinkle as if they had been inserted yesterday, and here and there a figure is executed almost too much in the modern manner to be interesting; for the charm of mosaic work is, to my sense, confined altogether to the infancy of the art. The great Christ, in the series of which I speak, is quite an elaborate picture, and yet he retains enough of the orthodox stiffness to make him impressive in the simpler, elder sense. He is clad in a purple robe, like an emperor, his hair and beard are artfully curled, his eyebrows arched, his complexion brilliant, his whole aspect such a one as the popular mind may have attributed to Honorius or Valentinian. It is all very Byzantine, and yet I found in it much of that interest which is inseparable, to a facile imagination, from all early representations of the Saviour. Practically, they are no more authentic than the more or less plausible inventions of Ary Scheffer and Holman Hunt; but they borrow a certain value, factitious perhaps but irresistible, from the mere fact that they are twelve or thirteen centuries less distant from the original. It is something that this is the way people in the sixth century imagined Jesus to have looked; the image is by so much the less complex. The great purple-robed monarch on the wall at Ravenna is at least a very potent and positive Christ, and the only objection I have to make to him is that, though in this character he must have had a full apportionment of divine foreknowledge, he betrays no apprehension of Dr. Channing and M. Renan. If one's preference lies, for distinctness' sake, between the old narrowness and the modern complexity, one must admit that the narrowness here has a very grand outline.

I spent the rest of the morning in picturesque transition between the hot, yellow streets and the cool, grey interiors of the churches. The greyness everywhere was lighted up by the scintillation, on vault and entablature, of mosaics more or less archaic, but always brilliant and elaborate, and everywhere, too, by the same keen wonderment that, while centuries had worn themselves away and empires risen and fallen, these little cubes of colored glass had stuck in their allotted places and kept their freshness. I have no space to enumerate the Ravennese churches one by one, and, to tell the truth, my memory of them has already become a sort of hazy confusion and formless meditation. The total aspect of Ravenna, its sepulchral stillness, its absorbing perfume of evanescence and decay and mortality, confounds the distinctions and blurs the details. The cathedral, which is very vast and high, has been excessively modernized, and was being still more so by a lavish application of tinsel and cotton-velvet in preparation for the centenary feast of St. Apollinaris, which befalls next month. Things on this occasion are to be done handsomely, and a fair Ravennese informed me that a single family had contributed three thousand francs towards a month's vesper-music. It seemed to me hereupon that I should like in the August twilight to wander into the quiet nave of San Apollinare, and look up at the great mosaics through the resonance of some fine chanting. I remember distinctly enough, however, the tall basilica of San Vitale, of octagonal shape, like an exchange or a custom-house—modelled, I believe, upon St. Sophia at Constantinople. It is very lofty, very solemn, and, as to the choir, densely pictured over on arch and apse with mosaics of the time of Justinian. These are regular pictures, full of movement, gesture, and perspective, and just enough sobered in hue by time to look historic and venerable. In the middle of the church, under the great dome, sat an artist whom I envied, making at an effective angle a picture of the choir and its broken lights, its decorated altar, and its encrusted, twinkling walls. The picture, when it is finished, will hang, I suppose, on the library wall of some person of taste; but even if it is much better than is probable (I didn't look at it), all his taste will not tell the owner, unless he has been there, in just what a soundless, mouldering, out-of-the-way corner of old Italy it was painted. An even better place for an artist fond of dusky architectural works, except that here the dusk is excessive and he would hardly be able to tell his green from his red, is the extraordinary little church of the Santi Nazaro e Celso, otherwise known as the mausoleum of Galla Placidia. This, perhaps, on the whole, is the most impressive and picturesque spot in Ravenna. It consists of a sort of narrow, low-browed cave, shaped like a Latin cross, every inch of which, except the floor, is covered with dense symbolic mosaics. Before you and on each side, through the thick, brown light, loom three enormous barbaric sarcophagi, containing the remains of potentates of the Lower Empire.

It is as if history had burrowed underground to escape from research, and you had fairly run it to earth. On the right lie the ashes of the Emperor Honorius, and in the middle those of his sister, Galla Placidia, a lady who I believe had great adventures. On the other side rest the bones of Constantius III. The place is like a little natural grotto lined with glimmering mineral substances, and there is something quite tremendous in being shut up so closely with these three imperial ghosts. The shadow of the great Roman name seems to tread upon the huge sepulchres and abide for ever within the narrow walls.

But there are other memories attached to Ravenna beside those of primitive bishops and degenerate emperors. Byron lived here and Dante died here, and the tomb of the one poet and the dwelling of the other are among the regular objects of interest. The grave of Dante, it must be said, is anything but Dantesque, and the whole precinct is disposed with that curious vulgarity of taste which distinguishes most modern Italian tributes to greatness. Dante memorialized in stucco, even in a slumbering corner of Ravenna, is not a satisfactory spectacle. Fortunately, of all poets he least needs a monument, as he was pre-eminently an architect in diction, and built himself his memorial in verses more solid than Cyclopean blocks. If Dante's tomb is not Dantesque, neither is Byron's house Byronic, being a homely, shabby, two-storied dwelling, directly on the street, with as little as possible of isolation and mystery. In Byron's time it was an inn, and it is rather a curious reflection that "Cain" and the "Vision of Judgment" should have been written at a hotel. Here is a commanding precedent as to self-abstraction for tourists who are at once sentimental and literary. I must declare, indeed, that my acquaintance with Ravenna considerably increased my esteem for Byron and helped to renew my faith in the sincerity of his inspiration. A man so much *de son temps* as Byron was, can have spent two long years in this profoundly stagnant city only by the help of taking a great deal of disinterested pleasure in his own genius. He had indeed a notable pastime (the various churches, by the way, are adorned with monuments of ancestral Guicciolis); but it is none the less obvious that Ravenna, fifty years ago, would have been an intolerably dull residence to a foreigner of distinction unprovided with a real intellectual passion. The hour one spends with Byron's memory, then, is a charitable one. After all, one says to one's self, as one turns away from the grandiloquent little slab in the front of his house and looks down the deadly provincial vista of the empty, sunny street, the author of so many superb stanzas asked less from the world than he gave to it. One of his diversions was to ride in the Pineta, which, beginning a couple of miles from the city, extends for some twenty-five miles along the sands of the Adriatic. I drove out to it for Byron's sake, and Dante's, and Boccaccio's, all of whom have interwoven it with their fictions, and for that of a possible whiff of coolness from the sea. Between the city and the forest, in the midst of malarious rice-swamps, stands the finest of the Ravenna churches, the stately temple of San Apollinare in Classe. The Emperor Augustus constructed hereabouts a harbor for fleets, which the ages have choked up, and which survives only in the title of this ancient church. Its extreme loneliness makes it doubly impressive. They opened the great doors for me, and let a shaft of heated air go wander up the beautiful nave, between the twenty-four lustrous, pearly columns of *cipollino* marble, and mount the wide staircase of the choir, and spend itself beneath the mosaics of the vault. I passed a delicious half-hour sitting there in this wave of tempered light, looking down the cool, grey avenue of the nave, out of the open door at the vivid green swamps, listening to the melancholy stillness. I rambled for an hour in the Pineta, between the tall, smooth, silvery stems of the pines, beside a creek which led me to the outer edge of the wood and a view of white sails, gleaming and gliding behind the sand-hills. It was infinitely picturesque; but, as the trees stand at wide intervals, and bear far aloft in the blue air but a little parasol of foliage, I suppose that, of a glaring summer day, the forest was only the more Italian for being perfectly shadeless.

LONDON SIGHTS

November 10, 1875

Albert Memorial, Kensington Gardens, ca. 1876.

WHEN THE ALBERT MEMORIAL WAS COMPLETED AND uncovered in London more than a year since, and displayed through the smoky air its treasures of florid architecture, there was much almost ribald jesting at the way the local atmosphere was destined to blight its gilding and its precious stones. The thing seemed like a sort of magnificent satire upon the

London climate. Some five years ago the beautiful new structure of the Royal Academy was brilliant with its carved white stone and its gleaming statues; to-day it is of a dusky, smutty gray, and to-morrow it will be as black and hoary as Westminster Abbey and St. Paul's. Having seen the Albert Memorial just after its erection, I was lately curious to observe whether its splendor had as yet begun perceptibly to wane. It must be confessed that up to this moment it has made a very successful resistance. It will have the best wishes of all lovers of the picturesque for its continued success; for whatever may be thought of its artistic merit or of the moral necessity for having erected it, it at least may be valued by the London wayfarers as the sole specimen of vivid color in the metropolis. Its position of course helps to preserve its purity, with the vast open spaces of Kensington Gardens beside it and behind it in one quarter, and the mitigated contaminations of the far-spreading terraces and crescents of Prince's Gate, Queen's Gate, etc., facing it on the other. Readers interested in these matters may be reminded that the Memorial stands on the edge of Kensington Gardens, opposite the great red-and-yellow rotunda of Albert Hall—a sort of utilitarian Coliseum, which, I believe, has not been found very useful. The Memorial is a wonderful combination of British sculpture and architecture, gilding, mosaic, and the work of the lapidary. It consists of an immense gilt canopy of Gothic design, under which an image of the Prince-Consort is destined to repose. It rises colossally from a huge embankment, as it were, of steps, at each corner of which is a group in marble representing one of the four great continents. The "motive" of these groups is sufficiently picturesque, a great local beast, of heroic proportions—the bull, the bison, the camel, and the elephant—being in each case the central figure; but the sculpture, like all the sculpture, is second-rate and common. It is the work, of course, of the highest English skill—of Messrs. Macdowell, Bell, Foley, and Theed. At each angle of the upper platform where the shafts of the canopy rise is another group— "Manufactures," by Mr. Weekes; "Commerce," by Mr. Thorney-croft; "Agriculture," by Mr. Marshall; and "Engineering," by Mr. Lawlor. Round this outer base of the canopy runs an immense frieze in white marble, executed half by Mr. Philip and half by Mr. Armstead, representing, a trifle below life-size, the array of the world's great artists—poets, painters, sculptors, musicians, and architects. They have been sagaciously chosen and cleverly combined, and the most expressive and original portion of the sculpture is here, we should say, especially on Mr. Armstead's side. As for the canopy itself, with its flamboyant Gothic, its columns of porphyry, its statues and statuettes of bronze and gold (or seem-ing gold), its chased and chiselled jeweller's-work, its radiant mo-saics, its thick-strewn gems of malachite and lapis and jasper and onyx and more rare stones than we know the names of, its gables and spires and pinnacles and crockets, its general gleaming and flashing and climbing and soaring, its great jewelled cross at the summit—all this quite beggars description. We should say in general that the workmanship throughout has been of a finer sort than the original taste, and that if the Memorial preserves in the future the memory of our present knowingness in architecture, it will also perpetuate the modern weakness of that art which once unfolded the friezes along the Parthenon and suspended the tombs in the Italian cathedrals.

The exhibition of paintings by Gustave Doré now on view in London ceased a good while since to demand notice as a novelty, but has become one of the regular sights of the great city, and it suggests some reflections that are always pertinent. The general air of the establishment is not so much that of a temple of the arts as of an enterprising place of business. The pictures seem to be placed on view chiefly with the design of securing subscribers to certain projected engravings. The agents for subscriptions are liberally diffused through the rooms, and as they mingle "quite promiscuous" (as the London vernacular has it) with the visitors, the latter are liable to be buttonholed in the midst of such attentive contemplation as Doré's canvases may have provoked. The engravings are to be executed in England, in the finest and smoothest style of the old-fashioned "line." It may very well be that the pictures will gain on being reduced to small dimensions and to simple black and white, for they look, as a general thing, like "illustrations" hugely magnified and rather crudely colored. The exhibition is of course an interesting one, and gives an extraordi-

nary impression of imagination, vigor, and facility. On the whole,
doubtless, one ought not to be afraid of enjoying it. We may be
tolerably sure that, where his pictures are wanting, M. Doré
knows it, that he has deliberately chosen to do only what he con-
veniently could, and that he has settled it in his mind that a magnificent effect, however obtained, is its own justification. The
artist's "convenience," we are at liberty to infer, has been to cover
an immense quantity of canvas and make a great deal of money.
As for his effects, the best of them are certainly magnificent. The
only valid criticism of Gustave Doré must rest, it seems to me, on
the admission that in the degree to which he possesses the temperament of the designer—in energy, and force, and consistency
of talent—he ranks with the few greatest names. He has a touch
of Michael Angelo about him; the fact that he is an enterprising
Parisian of the nineteenth century ought not to make this incon-
ceivable to us. In the power to compose an immense combination of figures at short notice he recalls two of his greatest
predecessors—Rubens and Tintoretto. We may prefer Rubens
and Tintoretto, and yet do justice to other members of the family. It is Doré's own fault if so often we find it very easy to prefer
them. He has chosen to work by wholesale, and so very often did
they, who, however, had the advantage that wholesale painting
in their times, owing to the essential tone of men's thoughts,
could not of necessity be so superficial as it may be to-day. Their
merit is that, whatever they did, they always achieved something

that may be called painting; and Doré's fault is that half the time his work is not painting at all. It is a rapid, superficial application of turbid and meaningless color—an imitation of painting not always particularly skillful. The two great things in London—the "Christ coming down from Judgment" and the "Tapis Vert"—are full of examples of this. The latter of these—a very cleverly imaginative representation of the gaming-table at Baden-Baden—is well known by photography, and known very favorably. The photograph flatters it, and so probably will the engraving, in giving it a charm of detail which the original lacks. The other picture—one of the largest ever painted—is full of imagination, skill, and power, and looks, as we intimated, like one of Doré's most successful drawings shown by a magic-lantern. It is a most extraordinary performance. The other pictures are full of cleverness and invention, especially certain "Christian Martyrs in the Coliseum," a heap of corpses lying in the empty arena, with wild beasts prowling over them in the blue starlight, and cold, phantasmal angels hovering above. The landscapes are singularly bad, many of them looking for all the world like second-rate American work. The best things have a merit which the way Doré has cheapened himself has made at last to seem trivial, but which would seem quite incomparable if it had been more abruptly presented. Their great fault is that they have no agreeable passages of painting—nothing exquisite, nothing that looks not only as if the artist had lingered over it, but as if he had even paused at it.

LONDON IN
THE DEAD SEASON
September 7, 1878

The great disaster on the Thames, ca. 1878.

T HERE ARE MOMENTS WHEN IT SEEMS TO SAVOR OF affectation to talk of London at any time as "empty"—to declare, in the language of the locality, that there is not a creature in town. But everything is relative, and it is not to be denied that at this time of the year the noisiest city in the world is apt to become peculiarly quiet. Bond Street is tranquil and

Piccadilly is soundless; the knocker is dumb in genteel neigh-
borhoods, the little double-tap of the postman even becomes
unfamiliar, and the ear is conscious only of the creaking boots
of the lonely policeman as he slowly marches through a vista of
darkened windows. I don't know how the policeman likes his
solitude and his leisure; but there is something about London in
its interlunar swoon, as Shelley says, which an occasional survi-
vor of the fashionable period finds decidedly agreeable. It may
be that as an adoptive rather than a native cockney I exaggerate
its charms at the present moment, according to the rule that
converts are always apt to be fanatics. If you like London for itself, as the phrase is, you get more of London itself at this time
than at any other. You enjoy a kind of monopoly of certain parts
of it, and you appreciate some of those great features which, at
any time from January to July, are thrown into the background
by the crowd and the bustle. I will not attempt to enumerate
the features in question, or suffer myself to be beguiled into an
attempt to demonstrate that among the gentle influences of
September the British metropolis takes on an unsuspected loveliness. One's enjoyment here at such a time must after all be
mainly, as the metaphysicians say, subjective. It comes from the
sense of boundless leisure—of the absence of interruptions. This
operates as a kindly revelation of the crowded quality of existence during the lively portion of the year. For a person leading,
in however small a degree, what is called a "London life," a fair,

smooth, open stretch of time—without visits or notes or social obligations—becomes the ideal of felicity.

If this ideal is realized at present, there are of course losses in the matter as well as gains. The London clubs, in the early autumn, betake themselves to house-cleaning; the familiar portal of your favorite resort is shut in your face, with the imperfect compensation of an announcement that for the next few weeks you are at liberty to make use of another establishment. At the other establishment you feel a good deal like an intruder: you are unfamiliar with the customs of the place—you imagine that the servants and members glower at you, as you go and come— you feel that there is a want of confidence in your deportment, that you are not welcomed, but only tolerated. In so far, however, as a club is a place for reading the papers, that at the present time is soon done; and if a gentleman should happen to want the copy of the *Times* which you have in hand you will not deprive him of it for many minutes. The morning journals are distinctly dull: in the absence of stirring intelligence the smallest contributions are thankfully received. That ingenious species of composition and product of our time, known as the "social article," receives particular attention; it is usually of a jocular cast and—once a text, or a pretext, is secured—is remarkable for the facility of its transitions. That characteristic of English manners which is supposed by strangers to be the leading one—the passion for "writing to the *Times*"—is at present a great godsend to that journal. I am ignorant whether the *Times* receives during the months of August and September a greater number of confidential epistles from the injured or the gratified, the disappointed, the swindled, the inquisitive, or the communicative Briton, but it certainly prints a great many more. One class of communications comes to it, of course, in especial abundance—the complaints of English travellers who are taking a holiday upon the Continent. There is a daily outpouring of grievances into the maternal bosom of the great newspaper; and I think there are few spectacles more striking and suggestive to a stranger. A stranger makes all kinds of reflections upon it, but he ends on the whole, decidedly, with admiring it. It is ridiculous, in many ways—sordid, egotistical, obtrusive; but it throws an interesting light upon that feature of the English character which is so intimately connected with the greatness of England—the stubborn sense of the rights of the individual. The English individual has not only a stronger, but a much more definite, conception of his rights than any other; he has a more definite and more cultivated notion of justice. It is this definiteness that is the striking point. Theoretically, an American has quite as lively a sense of his dues; but practically, politics apart, his notion of what these dues consist of is exceedingly vague and amateurish. An Englishman never hesitates; he has them at his fingers' ends. The magnitude of the infraction matters little; his comfort is as sensitive as his honor; the principle is sacred that the *other* part of the bargain—the part complementary to his own (which he has discharged by paying a certain sum of money or taking a certain course)—shall be performed rigidly and to the letter. No American who has known many Englishmen can have failed to be struck with the trouble his friends have often been willing to take for the redress of grievances which have seemed to him trifling and not worth time and temper; and many Englishmen, on the other hand, who have been acquainted with Americans, must often have been amazed at the good humor of the latter—the blank serenity, akin to the Mussulman's assent to fate—under imposition, delay, incivility. What is meant by "English comfort" is at bottom but this fixed standard of punctuality and of deference to the expectations of the consumer; and it is very certain that life is very comfortable—for consumers, of course—in a country where no offence against this standard is accounted venial.

I should give a very false impression of the current hour in London if I failed to say that for the last three days the newspapers have contained something very different from the usual complaints of leaking lamps in railway carriages and of the heavy boots worn at night in the corridors of Swiss hotels. A very terrible accident occurred on the 3d ult. on the Thames— an accident which has added a peculiar gloom to the actual soberness of London. A small, overcrowded steamer, returning from an excursion to Gravesend, was run down by a big collier and sunk in an instant, with seven hundred persons on board. This huge calamity will, of course, long since have been made known in America, and you will have been spared those horrible details in which the voluminous reports published here abound. The collision took place just above Woolwich, and the latest computation appears to be that six hundred persons have perished. I have, at various idle moments, found entertainment in a sixpenny steamer, and may almost claim familiarity with that dusky stretch of the Thames which lies between Woolwich and London. The adoptive cockney, of whom I spoke just now, feels a curiosity to sound the depths of metropolitan amusement, and he has been known, under the guidance of this feeling, to push his researches even as far as Gravesend—a very shabby resort of pleasure, now for some time to be associated with the hideous disaster of three days since. The Thames scenery between London and Gravesend is anything but beautiful, but it has always seemed to me to have a certain sordid picturesqueness. There was entertainment to the eye in the dusky, irregular waterside, which seemed to stand begging to be "etched," and in the large, turbid, crowded river, with the slow-moving vessels almost fixed in it, as if it were liquid glue. The place seemed dingy and dreary, but it never seemed tragical—any more than the participants in a Gravesend excursion looked like actors in a tragedy.

I can speak of such an assemblage from observation, for on a certain hot Sunday, some time ago, I found myself in the midst of one. Partly as an enquiring stranger and partly as the victim of a misconception of the attractions of Gravesend I went to the latter place by train, to take the air. After taking as much of it as seemed agreeable, I returned to London with a very big crowd on a very small boat—the same rotten little steamer, possibly, which collapsed at a touch the other night. In so far as my expedition served as a study of the manners of the British populace it was highly successful, and the objects of that study have remained vividly imprinted on my memory. Gravesend itself can best be described by an expression borrowed from the feminine vocabulary: it is simply too dreadful. It is an extremely dirty and most ingeniously vulgar little place, close upon the river, whose bank is adorned with a row of small establishments, half cottage and half shop, devoted to traffic in shrimps and tea. The doors of these little tea-houses are garnished with terrible maidens—very stout and robust, high-colored and loud-voiced—who dart forth at the wayfarer, tea-pot in hand, and, vociferating in his ears certain local formulas, almost hustle him into their unappetizing bowers. Behind the town is a place of entertainment known as the Rosherville Gardens, where there are more conveniences of the kind I have described, together with a hundred others in the way of rock-work and plaster statues and convivial grottoes. The British populace, returning from what the advertisements call a "happy day" at Rosherville, struck me, on the steamer, rather less favorably than an adoptive cockney could have wished. I had nothing to do for a couple of hours but to sit upon the paddle-box and watch it; but there was no great charm in the spectacle. The "people" in certain foreign countries, notably in France and Italy, is a decidedly more remunerative spectacle than the moneyed class. It strikes one as containing more than half the vivacity and originality of the nation. But this is far from being the case here. There is something particularly coarse and dusky about an English mob, something which is not redeemed even by its great good-nature, and which comes, I think, in a great measure from the absence of the look of taste and thrift in the women. I don't know, however, that this reflection is at all pertinent to the horrible disaster which occurred last Tuesday, and which has made, for the week, a kind of charnel-house of all the Woolwich shore. With all its imperfections on its head, a very considerable group of the London populace was cruelly submerged. There will be an enquiry and a good deal of sensational reporting, and then the whole episode will sink beneath the surface as the boatload of excursionists sank. Meanwhile the grouse-shooting and the destruction of pheasants and partridges will proceed apace. A very large number of Englishmen are just now engaged in this pastime, and in the great stillness of London you can almost hear the crack of the fowling-pieces on the northern moors. A great many legislators are within earshot of this delightful sound; a few others are listening to the even sweeter music of their own voices. The *Times* has a regular corner devoted to Parliament out of session, which has lately contained several long speeches from honorable members to their constituents. But for the moment the public mind—or, at any rate, the private mind—is not political.

IN SCOTLAND

September 1878

*Princes Street and castle from
Scott's Monument, Edinburgh, ca. 1890.*

I. SEPTEMBER 25, 1878

Now that the metropolis is so inanimate I hardly need apologize
to you for writing from a livelier place than London. It is not
making an exorbitant claim for Edinburgh to say that at present
it deserves this description, for it has simply gained by the departed life of its sister capital. This afternoon, with a military
band playing in the long green garden below Princes Street, in

the shadow of the magnificent mass of the Castle Rock, with a host of well-dressed people collected to listen to the music; with the brilliant terrace above adorned with prosperous hotels and besprinkled with tourists divided between the attractions of shop-fronts and the striking picture formed by the Old Town and its high-perched citadel—this admirable Edinburgh looked like a very merry place. Scotland is a highly convenient play-ground for English idlers, and Edinburgh, during the early autumn, comes in for a great deal of the bustle produced by the ebb of the southern tide. For the last six weeks this annual current has been irrigating (not to say irritating) the Scottish moors and mountains; and it is hardly too much to say that at this period you must come to Scotland to see what England is about.

When I came hither myself, a little more than a fortnight ago, there were still plenty of members of the large class which has autumnal leisure to spare, hurrying northward. The railway-carriages were occupied, and the platforms of the stations orna-mented, by ladies and gentlemen in shooting-jackets of every pattern and hue. I say "ladies" advisedly, for the fairer members of these groups had every appearance of being sporting charac-ters. I do not know what may be the feminine costume of this particular period in America, but here it consists of a billycock hat with a very small brim, a standing collar of a striped or fig-ured linen, like that belonging to a "fancy" shirt, a scarf in a sailor's knot, a coachman's overcoat, made of some cross-barred material like the nether integuments of a "nigger-minstrel," and a petticoat clinging as closely as a pair of tight trousers and effectually completing the illusion. The proper accessories of such a figure are a gentleman draped rather more redundantly, and an aggregation of luggage consisting of a good many baskets and bath-tubs, of several *fasces* of fishing-rods, and divers gun-cases that look like carpet-bags flattened and elongated by steam-pressure; the whole set off by a couple of delightful setters or retrievers fastened to the handle of a trunk, and, amid the bustle of the railway-platform, turning themselves about and sniffing at this and that in touching bewilderment. A friend of mine, an American, was once asked to mention the two features of English life which had made most impression on him. He hesitated a moment, and then he said, "The dogs and the children." The children apart, it is worth coming to Scotland simply to encounter the very flower of the canine race—the beautiful silken-eared animals that follow in the train of the happy Englishmen who have hired a moor at a thousand pounds for six weeks' grouse-shooting. England is certainly the paradise of dogs; nowhere are they better appreciated and understood. But Scotland is their seventh heaven. Of course all the Englishmen who cross the Tweed have not paid a thousand pounds down as the basis of their entertainment, though the number of gentlemen who have permitted themselves this fancy appears to be astonishing. Tourists of the more vulgar pattern, who have simply come to enjoy the beauties of nature and to read the quotations, in the guide-books, from Sir Walter Scott, are extremely numerous, and Scotland, as regards some of the provisions that she makes for them, takes on the air of a humbler Switzerland. One must admit, however, that though the Scotch inns are much better than the English, they do not push their easy triumph very far; they bear the same relation to the Swiss hotels that the scenery of the Highlands does to that of the Alps. But if their merits are not unalloyed, it is not for want of resolution—as, for instance, in the matter of the table d'hôte. The table d'hôte in the British Islands is essentially an importation, an exotic, a drooping and insalubrious flame. But like all new converts the Scotch inn-keepers are immoderate; they are of the opinion that of a good thing there can never be too much. A couple of days since, at Stirling, I was invited to be present at a table d'hôte at half-past eight a.m. The idea was sufficient to make the bodies of Meurice and Francatelli turn over in their graves. I am bound to admit, however, that I countenanced this matutinal heresy by my presence; and I again had occasion to reflect upon the extreme punctuality with which, in the British organism, the desire for copious supplies of animal food asserts itself. A week ago, at a table d'hôte at Ballater, just after the company had seated itself, there came a great thump at the head of the table—a rap which caused me to start with the apprehension that I had inadvertently introduced myself into a spiritualistic *séance*. I was speedily reassured—a gentleman growled out a "grace." Nothing, in effect, could have been less spiritual than this performance; but I wondered what, even from a material point of view, the shades of Francatelli and Meurice thought of it.

"This admirable Edinburgh," I said just now; and I must venture to emphasize the fresh approbation of a susceptible stranger. The night of my arrival here was a superb one; the full moon had possession of a cloudless sky. I saw, on my way from the station, that it was working wonders on some very remunerative material; so that after a very brief delay I came forth into the street, and presently wandered all over the place. There is no street in Europe more spectacular than Princes Street, where all the hotels stand in a row, looking off, across the long green gulf that divides the New Town from the Old, at the dark, rugged mass of the latter section. But on the evening of which I speak Princes Street was absolutely operatic. The radiant moon hung right above the Castle and the ancient houses that keep it company on its rocky pedestal, and painted them over with a thousand silvery, ghostly touches. They looked fantastic and ethereal, like the battlements of a magician's palace. I had not gone many steps from my hotel before I encountered the big gothic monument to Scott, which rises on the edge of the terrace into which Princes Street practically resolves itself. Viewing it in the broad daylight of good taste, I am not sure that I greatly care for this architectural effort, which, as all the world knows, consists of a colossal canopy erected above a small seated image of the great romancer. It looks a little too much like a steeple without a church, or like a hat a great deal too big for the head it covers. But the other night, in the flattering moonlight, it presented itself in all respects so favorably that I found myself distinctly what the French call ému, and said to myself that it was a grand thing to have deserved so well of one's native town that she should build a towering temple in one's honor. Sir Walter's great canopy is certainly an object which a member of the scribbling fraternity may contemplate with a sort of reflex complacency. I carried my reflex complacency—a rather awkward load—up the Calton Hill, whose queer jumble of monuments and colonnades looked really sublime in the luminous night, and then I descended into the valley and watched the low, black mass of Holyrood Palace sleeping in its lonely outlying corner, where Salisbury Crags and Arthur's Seat seemed rather to lose than to define themselves in the clarified dusk. The sight of all this really splendid picturesqueness suggested something that has occurred to me more than once since I have been in Scotland—the idea, namely, that if that fine quality of Scotch conceit which, if I mistake not, all the world recognizes, is, as I take it to be, the most robust thing of its kind in the world, the wonder after all is not great. I have said to myself during the last fortnight that if I were a Scotchman I too should be conceited, and that I should especially avail myself of this privilege if I were a native of Edinburgh.

I should be proud of a great many things. I should be proud of belonging to a country whose capital is one of the most romantic and picturesque in Europe. I should be proud of Scott and Burns, of Wallace and Bruce, of Mary Stuart and John Knox, of the tremendously long list of Scotch battles and heroic deeds. I should brag about the purple of the heather and the colors of the moors, and I should borrow a confidence (which indeed I should be far from needing) from the bold, masculine beauty of my native mountains. Above all, I should take comfort in belonging to a country in which natural beauty and historical association are blended only less perfectly than they are blended in Italy and Greece; whose physiognomy is so intensely individual and homogeneous, and, as the artists say, has so much style.

I am afraid, however, that I am sketching here a fancy picture of Scottish conceit; the chief characteristic of this great gift being its extreme independence—the fact that it is much more personal than national. An Englishman believes in England and a Frenchman in France, but a Scotchman believes in—a Scotchman. The acute Scotch intellect—the *perfervidum ingenium*—believes in itself. Of the frankness with which it can acknowledge national shortcomings I find an interesting example in a speech which Principal Shairp, of St. Andrew's, who was lately the successful candidate for the chair of Poetry at Oxford, has just had occasion to deliver at Edinburgh. The main subject of his remarks was the existing defects in some portions of the present

Scotch educational system; but before he had done he devoted some observations to a cognate topic—the tone of Scotch manners. These he described as rather rough and rude, dry and wanting in urbanity; and he attributed the defect to the influence of those two principles which he declared to be paramount on this side of the Tweed—sectarianism and the love of money. "Mr. Matthew Arnold had spoken of the uncivilizedness of Glasgow. That was strong language; but he dared not deny it when he remembered what he himself had seen in walking down the High Street of Glasgow on a Saturday night—a spectacle of human hideousness of which, he believed, no other civilized country could produce a parallel." Among various remedies for this state of things Principal Shairp, as befits a professor of poetry, recommends the perusal of the great bards and the cultivation of music. I am afraid the poets and singers would quite lose their way in Glasgow High Street. It is not for a visitor who has received none but delightful impressions to pretend to agree with Principal Shairp; but there is nothing invidious in saying that an American coming into Scotland after a residence in England cannot fail to be struck with the democratic tone of the common people. They address you as from equal to equal, they are not in the least cap-in-hand, and they are frugal—almost miserly—in the use of the "sir." This is as good a basis of good manners as any other, though of course one can't answer for it when Principal Shairp's "sectarianism" comes in. But I have really no business even to quote such expressions. I have encountered in Scotland but a single sect—the sect whose religion is hospitality.

II. September 30, 1878

There are two things in England in regard to which I think it safe to say that a stranger, however familiar he may become with English life, remains always a stranger—always uninitiated, profane, and even more or less indifferent. One of these matters is—with all respect be it written—the internal dissensions and perplexities of the Anglican Church. This remarkable body strikes the pure outsider so much more as a social than as a religious institution that he feels inclined to say to himself that these are purely local and national mysteries, and that, so far as he is concerned, they may be left to take care of themselves. The other point is the great British passion for sport—the deepest and most general of all British passions. This, in England, is the touch of nature that makes the whole world kin. A person from another country may have a lively enjoyment of riding, shooting, rowing; but in face of the tremendous cohesiveness of the sporting interest in England he feels that to care for such things as these people do, one must be to the manner born. It will seem to him at times that they care too much, and he will, perhaps, embark upon that interesting line of enquiry, at what particular point the love of physical exercise becomes stultifying. It behooves him to remember, however, that there is one particular way in which the sporting interest in England is humanizing. It is the subject on which the greatest number of Englishmen, at a given moment, can feel together; it is the thing which, as M. Thiers said of the French Republic, divides them least. It serves as a bond of union, as a patch of common ground, in a country extraordinarily cut up by social distinctions; it introduces the leaven of democracy into the most aristocratically constituted society in the world. On the receipt of the latest intelligence from Newmarket a "cad" may feel very much like a lord; I won't, indeed, go so far as to say that a lord may feel like a cad.

What I intended especially to say was that a fortnight spent in Scotland is to the alien mind a kind of revelation of the part allotted to physical recreation in a well-arranged English life. It is very true that I am unable to add that in this particular case the democratic bearings of the fact are noticeable. Scotland, for the late summer and autumn, becomes an immense "shooting." It is excellently arranged for the purpose, and its purple moors and heathery hillsides resolve themselves into the last luxury of a supremely luxurious class. This is the real identity of the various elements of the beautiful Scottish scenery. The uninitiated eye sees nothing but a lovely purple mountain or a blushing moor, adorned with the advantages of aerial perspective. But in its essential and individual character such a piece of landscape is

Mr. So-and-So's deer-forest (a deer-forest by no means implies trees) or Lord Such-a-One's provision of grouse. There is something very singular in the part played by Scotland nowadays— the small number of proprietors of the territory, the immense extent of the estates, and the fact that these exist almost wholly for purposes of recreation. I spoke the other day of a Scotchman's just grounds for national pride; but it is fair to add that just here this tendency might perhaps encounter an obstacle. It seems to me that if I were a fervid Caledonian I should find something irritating, and even mortifying, in the sight of my beautiful little country parcelled out, on so immense a scale, into playgrounds for English millionaires. Was it for this that my ancestors bled with Wallace or flocked about Bruce? Doubtless, however, this is an idle line of speculation, for the moors and hillsides are apparently better for playgrounds than for anything else, and if the Sassenach has money to pay for them it is hard to see how he is to be prevented. In the south of Scotland (in Dumfriesshire) a friend with whom I was walking led me up to a hilltop and showed me a remarkable view. The country seemed of immense extent—it consisted of innumerable grassy sheepdowns—and the blue horizon looked ever so far away. The afternoon light was slanting over the long undulations and dying away in the distance; the whole region looked like a little kingdom. "It's all the Duke's," said my friend—"this, twenty miles away, and ever so much besides." In every Scotch or English county there is a personage known as "the Duke" *par excellence*. This fortunate mortal, in the present case, was the Duke of Buccleuch, upon whose remarkable merits as a landlord my companion proceeded to expatiate. What I saw of the Duke's kingdom seemed an admirable grazing country: but elsewhere my observation was confined to picturesque expanses of rock-scattered heath. Even if they were keeping a superior sort of exploitation at bay, it would be hard, from their own point of view, to blame the deer-stalking and grouse-shooting gentry. I speak not even from the point of view of a sportsman, but simply from that of an unarmed promenader stepping across the elastic heather on a brilliant September morning. On such an occasion the admirable freshness of the Scotch air, the glory of the light and color, the absence from the landscape of economical suggestions, appear to be equal parts of one's entertainment.

This absence of economical suggestions does not in the least mean, however, that the happy residents on a Scotch moor are obliged to rough it. The English, who arrange their lives everywhere so well, arrange them nowhere better than in Scotland. It is indeed, in many cases, simply Mayfair among the heather. From the point of view of a purely Wordsworthian love of nature, a shooting-lodge with ball-room may appear an anomaly; but I encountered this phenomenon in the midst of a Scotch deer-forest. The ball-room, too, was in full operation, and the national dance—the Highland reel—in course of performance. The ladies and gentlemen engaged in this choreographic revel were by no means all, or even preponderantly, native—a fact which may account for the vivacity of their movements, inasmuch as we know that proselytes are always more violent than the natural heirs of a tradition. Apart, however, from its suggesting that the Highland kilt is an odd sort of garment for ceremonial purposes and the sanctity of the English after-dinner period, the Scotch reel, with its leapings and hootings, its liftings of the leg and brandishings of the arm, is a very pretty country-house frolic. A stranger, looking for local color in everything, finds a great deal of it here; and he pays a compliment, moreover, to the muscular resources and good spirits of those young Englishmen who can dance till three o'clock in the morning after tramping over the moors all day with a gun. Like a good many other things, the reel has doubtless suffered by the conversion of the Highlanders into an adjunct of Piccadilly. Among the things that have suffered, I believe, are the old Highland sports, from which it was intimated to me that the good faith and the ancient cunning had departed. Though it was further intimated to me that one must be a deplorable cockney to be still taken in by them. I ventured to find a great deal of entertainment in what I saw of them. There was certainly one occasion with which it was impossible not to be charmed, including as it did a capital collation under a graceful marquee, not at all crowded, on the edge of a great green meadow that was circled about with hills. Through the front of the tent, largely looped up, one saw the bright-colored little crowd sitting about on the grass, and in the midst, on a platform, a series of Highlanders, one by one, with their great tartans flying, jumping about in the figures of the sword-dance. And then there were leaping and tugging and hurdle-racing and a little tournament of bag-pipes. The lively drone of this instrument came in from the distance with the summer breeze; far away, as an undertone to agreeable talk, it was not unpleasant. I was annoyed at being told the Highlanders were "cads"; and indeed, on a nearer view, they had a rather jaded and histrionic look. But if the play was a comedy, it was a very successful one.

There are some other old Scottish institutions which have retained their vitality and are apparently in very good repair. The Caledonian "Sawbath," I believe, still flourishes, and I am told that in Edinburgh and Aberdeen it may be observed in high perfection. I had a glimpse of it, only in the country, where it was mitigated by the charming scenery, which remained persistently and profanely bright. But it was very ugly; it was grotesquely ugly. There was a horrible little kirk on a windy hillside equally naked without and within—except, indeed, as regards such internal warmth as was supplied by the deportment of a rustic congregation listening in almost voracious silence and immobility to a doctrine addressed to violent theological appetites. My host had recommended me to attend this service (which was an excellent example of grim Presbyterianism) for local color's sake; and certainly the little exhibition was very complete. The strange compound produced in the sermon by the profusion of Jewish names and of Scotch accents; the air of doctrinal vigilance on the part of the cautious, dry-faced auditory; the crude, nasal singing; the rapid dispersal afterwards, over the stony hillsides to their rugged little cottages, of a congregation for which this occasion represented the imaginative side of life, as if the native granite had given it out and had immediately reabsorbed it—all this had at least a character of its own.

Old Scotland survives, however, fortunately, in more graceful forms than this. There is one advantage which European life will long have over American—the opportunity that it affords for going to picnic in the shadow of ancient castles. Given one of those Franco-Scottish fortified dwellings which sprang up so thickly under the influence of that long union between Scotland and France which was produced by their having an enemy in common; given, moreover, one of those admirable English lunch-hampers which, as it exposes its ingenious receptacles to view, the passing stranger pauses to admire in the shop-windows of Piccadilly; given in connection with this instrument a British butler's punctual performance of familiar duties; given, finally, a stretch of greensward, a group of bushes, a peeping above them of grey old towers and battlements, a charming company, and you have the elements of one of the most agreeable episodes of a sojourn beyond the Tweed. Some of the old foreign-looking

Scotch castles are admirable; there are very few of them that would not seem very much more in their proper place in France or Germany than in Scotland. The Scotch nobility, before the son of Mary Stuart came to the English throne, must have been intensely Gallicized; the taste for French forms is visible in every detail of their domestic architecture. The old *poivrière*— the "pepper-pot" turret—is almost universal, and the very material of the edifice is Continental. In England it is a very rare thing to find an old manor-house covered with stucco or untimbered plaster; it is almost invariably of honest brick or stone. There is plenty of stucco in English street-architecture, but our own ingenious period must have the credit of it. In Scotland it abounds on the tall sides of the old domiciliary fortresses. One of these interesting monuments struck me as more than French—it was absolutely Italian. On its roof, in the midst of its gables and turrets, it had a couple of balustraded loggias, such as you see in very old Italian villas; and the resemblance was carried out by the large, windowless expanses of grey, rugged, sun-baked plaster on the walls. There is something decidedly Continental, too, in the older portions of the Scotch towns. I except the granitic Aberdeen and the industrial Glasgow; but nothing is less recognizably British than the high-piled, unconventional Edinburgh. The other evening, at Stirling, taking a stroll at hazard, I encountered a *porte-cochére*.

THE LONDON THEATRES
May 24, 1879

Theatre Royal, Drury Lane, ca. 1813.

M R. MATTHEW ARNOLD, IN HIS VOLUME OF "MIXED Essays," lately published, in speaking somewhere of some of the less creditable features of English civilization, alludes to the British theatre as "probably the most contemptible in Europe." The judgment is a harsh one, but he would be a bold man who, looking round him at the condition of the London stage at the present moment, should attempt to gainsay it. I have lately made a point of gathering such impressions on the subject as were easily obtainable, and a brief record of them may not be without interest. The first impression one receives in England on turning one's attention at all in this direction, is that a very large number of people are doing the same. The theatre just now is the fashion, just as "art" is the fashion and just as literature is not. The English stage has probably never been so bad as it is at present, and at the same time there probably has never been so much care about it. It sometimes seems to an observer of English customs that this interest in histrionic matters almost reaches the proportions of a mania. It pervades society—it breaks down barriers. If you go to an evening party, nothing is more probable than that all of a sudden a young lady or a young gentleman will jump up and strike an attitude and begin to recite a poem or a speech. Every pretext for this sort of exhibition is ardently cultivated, and the London world is apparently filled with stage-struck young persons whose relatives are holding them back from a dramatic career by the skirts of their garments. Plays and actors are perpetually talked about, private theatricals are incessant, and members of the dramatic profession are "received" without restriction. They appear in society, and the people of society appear on the stage; it is as if the great gate which formerly divided the theatre from the world had been lifted off its hinges. There is, at any rate, such a passing to and fro as has never before been known; the stage has become amateurish and society has become professional. There are various explanations of this state of things, of which I am far from expressing disapproval; I mention it only because, superficially, it might seem that the theatre would have drawn strength from this large development of public favor. It is part of a great general change which has come over English manners—of the confusion of many things which forty years ago were kept very distinct. The world is being steadily democratized and vulgarized, and literature and art give their testimony to the fact. The fact is better for the world perhaps, but I question greatly whether it is better for art and literature; and therefore it is that I was careful to say just now that it is only *superficially* that one might expect to see the stage elevated by becoming what is called the fashion. They are in the truth of the matter very much more in France. In France, too, the democratizing, vulgarizing movement, the confusion of kinds, is sufficiently perceptible; but the stage has still, and will probably long have, the good fortune of not becoming the fashion. It is something at once more and less than the fashion, and something more respectable and permanent, and a part of the national life. It is a need, a constant habit, enjoying no fluctuations of credit. The French esteem the theatre too much to take rash liberties with it, and they have a wholesome dread, very natural in an artistic people, of abusing the source of their highest pleasure. Recitations, readings, private theatricals, public experiments by amateurs who have fallen in love with the footlights, are very much less common in France than in England, and of course still less common in the United States. Another fact that helps these diversions to flourish in England is the immense size of society, the prevalence of country life, the existence of an enormous class of people who have nothing in the world to do. The famous "leisure class," which is the envy and admiration of so many good Americans, has certainly invented a great many expedients for getting through the time; but there still remains for this interesting section of the human race a considerable danger of being bored, and it is to escape this danger that many of the victims of leisure take refuge in playing at histrionics.

In France (as I spoke just now of France) the actor's art, like the ancient arts and trades, is still something of a "mystery"—a thing of technical secrets, of special knowledge. This kind of feeling about it is inevitably much infringed when it becomes the fashion, in the sense that I have alluded to, and certainly the evidences of training—of a school, a discipline, a body of science—are on the English stage conspicuous by their absence. Of how little the public taste misses these things or perceives the need of them, the great and continued success of Mr. Henry Irving is a striking example. I shall not here pretend to judge Mr. Irving; but I may at least say that even his most ardent admirers would probably admit that he is an altogether irregular performer, and that an artistic education has had little to do with the results that he presents to the public. I do not mean by this, of course, that he has not had plenty of practice; I mean simply that he is an actor who, in default of any help rendered him, any control offered him by the public taste, by an ideal in the public mind, has had to get himself together and keep himself together as he could. He is at present the principal "actuality" of the London stage, and his prosperity has taken a fresh start with his having at the beginning of the winter established a theatre of his own and obtained the graceful assistance of Miss Ellen Terry. I say I shall not pretend to judge Mr. Irving, because I am aware that I must in the nature of the case probably do him injustice. His starting-point is so perfectly opposed to any that I find conceivable that it would be idle to attempt to appreciate him. In the opinion of many people the basis, the prime condition, of acting is the art of finished and beautiful utterance— the art of speaking, of saying, of diction, as the French call it; and such persons find it impossible to initiate themselves into any theory of the business which leaves this out of account. Mr. Irving's theory eliminates it altogether, and there is perhaps a great deal to be said for his point of view. I must, however, leave the task of elucidating it to other hands. He began the present season with a revival of "Hamlet"—a part, one would say, offering peculiar obstacles to treatment on this system of the unimportance of giving value to the text; and now, for some weeks past, he has been playing the "Lady of Lyons" with great success. To this success Miss Ellen Terry has very considerably contributed. She is greatly the fashion at present, and she belongs properly to a period which takes a strong interest in aesthetic furniture, archaeological attire, and blue china. Miss Ellen Terry is "aesthetic"; not only her garments but her features themselves bear the stamp of the new enthusiasm. She has a charm, a great deal of a certain amateurish, angular grace, a total want of what the French call *chic*, and a countenance very happily adapted to the expression of pathetic emotion. To this last effect her voice also contributes; it has a sort of monotonous husky thickness which is extremely touching, though it gravely interferes with the modulation of many of her speeches. Miss Terry, however, to my sense, is far from having the large manner, the style and finish, of a *comédienne*. She is the most pleasing and picturesque figure upon the English stage, but the other night, as I sat watching the "Lady of Lyons," I said to myself that her charming aspect hardly availed to redeem the strange, dingy grotesqueness of that decidedly infelicitous drama.

The two best theatres in London are the Court and the Prince of Wales's, and the intelligent playgoer is supposed chiefly to concern himself with what takes place at these houses. It is certainly true that at either house you see the London stage at its best; they possess respectively the two most finished English actors with whom I am acquainted. Mr. Arthur Cecil, at the Prince of Wales's, has a ripeness and perfection of method which reminds me of the high finish of the best French acting. He is an artist in very much the same sense that Got and Coquelin are artists. The same may be said of Mr. Hare at the Court, whose touch is wonderfully light and unerring. Indeed, for a certain sort of minute, almost painter-like elaboration of a part that really suits him, Mr. Hare is very remarkable. But the merits of these two actors, and those of some of their comrades at either theatre, only serve to throw into relief the essential weakness of the whole institution—the absolute poverty of its repertory. When Matthew Arnold speaks of the "contemptible" character of the contemporary English theatre, he points of course not merely at the bad acting which is so largely found there; he alludes also to its perfect literary nudity. Why it is that in the English language of our day there is not so much even as an unsuccessful attempt at a dramatic literature—such as is so largely visible in Germany and Italy, where "original" plays, even though they be bad ones, are produced by the hundred—this is quite a question by itself, and one that it would take some space to glance at. But it is sufficiently obvious that the poverty of the modern English theatre is complete, and it is equally obvious that the theatre is all one—that the drama and the stage hold together. There can be no serious school of acting unless there is a dramatic literature to feed it; the two things act and react upon each other—they are a reciprocal inspiration and encouragement. Anything less inspiring than the borrowed wares, vulgarized and distorted in the borrowing, upon which the English stage of to-day subsists, cannot well be imagined. Coarse adaptations of French comedies, with their literary savor completely evaporated, and their form and proportions quite sacrificed to the queer obeisances they are obliged to make to that incongruous phantom of a morality which has not wit enough to provide itself with an entertainment conceived in its own image—this is the material on which the actor's spirit is obliged to exert itself. The result is natural enough, and the plays and the acting are equally crude.

There can be no better proof of the poverty of the repertory than the expedients to which the Court and the Prince of Wales's have been reduced during the present winter. The Court has been playing a couple of threadbare French pieces of twenty and thirty years ago—a stiff translation of Scribe's "Bataille de Dames," and a commonplace version of a commonplace drama entitled "Le Fils de Famille." Scribe's piece is a clever light comedy—it is still sometimes played at the Théâtre Français; but it belongs at this time of day quite to the dramatic scrap-bag. There is something pitiful in seeing it dragged into the breach and made to figure for weeks as the stock entertainment at one of the two best English theatres. At the Prince of Wales's they have been playing all winter and are still playing Robertson's "Caste"—a piece of which, in common with the other productions of the same hand, it is only possible to say that it belongs quite to the primitive stage of dramatic literature. It is the infancy of art; it might have been written by a clever under-teacher for representation at a boarding-school. At the Criterion there is a comedy entitled "Truth," by an American author, Mr. Bronson Howard. Even the desire to speak well of American productions is insufficient to enable me to say that Mr. Bronson Howard offers a partial contradiction to Matthew Arnold's dictum. "Truth" may be an "original" drama; I know nothing of its history; but it produces the effect of the faint ghost of any old conventional French vaudeville—the first comer—completely divested of intellectual garniture, reduced to its simplest expression, and diluted in British propriety.

ILLUSTRATION CREDITS

157   Side view of the Bad Homburg von der Höhe palace, ca. 1860. Library of Congress.

171   The castle of Darmstadt in Hessen, Germany. Seen from the West, ca. 1900. Wikimedia.

185   A view of Florence from the Arno. New York Public Library Digital Collections.

197   Cathedral Square, Pisa, Italy. Library of Congress.

211   The building commonly known as the Mausoleum of Galla Placidia in Ravenna, in a drawing by Harald Sund, ca. 1910.

225   Albert Memorial, Kensington Gardens, ca. 1876. Flickr, via Cornell Library.

231   The great disaster on the Thames: Collision between the *Princess Alice* and the *Bywell Castle,* near Wollwich, ca. 1878. Wikimedia.

241   Princes Street and castle from Scott's Monument, Edinburgh, ca. 1890. Library of Congress.

257   Theatre Royal, Drury Lane, ca. 1813. Wikimedia.

INDEX

Henry James (1843–1916) is the author of such classic novels as *The Portrait of a Lady*, *The Turn of the Screw*, *Daisy Miller*, *The Golden Bowl*, and *Washington Square*.

Photo from the frontispiece of *Short Story Classics (American)*, *Volume Three*, ed. William Patten, copyright © 1905, printed by P.F. Collier & Son. Photographer unknown. *Wikimedia*.

The Nation Institute

Founded in 2000, **Nation Books** has become a leading voice in American independent publishing. The imprint's mission is to tell stories that inform and empower just as they inspire or entertain readers. We publish award-winning and bestselling journalists, thought leaders, whistleblowers, and truthtellers, and we are also committed to seeking out a new generation of emerging writers, particularly voices from underrepresented communities and writers from diverse backgrounds. As a publisher with a focused list, we work closely with all our authors to ensure that their books have broad and lasting impact. With each of our books we aim to constructively affect and amplify cultural and political discourse and to engender positive social change.

Nation Books is a project of The Nation Institute, a nonprofit media center established to extend the reach of democratic ideals and strengthen the independent press. The Nation Institute is home to a dynamic range of programs: the award-winning Investigative Fund, which supports groundbreaking investigative journalism; the widely read and syndicated website TomDispatch; journalism fellowships that support and cultivate over twenty-five emerging and high-profile reporters each year; and the Victor S. Navasky Internship Program.

For more information on Nation Books and The Nation Institute, please visit:

www.nationbooks.org
www.nationinstitute.org
www.facebook.com/nationbooks.ny
Twitter: @nationbooks